THE DISCIPLINE OF EDUCATION

The DISCIPLINE *of* EDUCATION

EDITED BY

John Walton

AND

James L. Kuethe

THE UNIVERSITY OF WISCONSIN PRESS

MADISON, 1963

PUBLISHED BY
The University of Wisconsin Press
430 Sterling Court, Madison 6, Wisconsin

Copyright © 1963 by the
Regents of the University of Wisconsin
Printed in the United States of America by
Vail-Ballou Press Inc., Binghamton, New York

Library of Congress Catalog Card Number 63-19212

CONTRIBUTORS

BERNARD BAILYN *Professor of History, Harvard University*

JOHN B. CARROLL *Roy Edward Larsen Professor of Educational Psychology and Director of the Laboratory for Research in Instruction, Graduate School of Education, Harvard University*

JAMES S. COLEMAN *Professor and Chairman, Department of Social Relations, Johns Hopkins University*

JAMES DEESE *Professor of Psychology, Johns Hopkins University*

EVERETT C. HUGHES *Professor of Sociology, Brandeis University*

JAMES L. KUETHE *Associate Professor of Education, Johns Hopkins University*

JAMES E. McCLELLAN *Professor and Director of the Department of Foundations of Education, Temple University*

R. S. PETERS *Professor of Philosophy of Education, Institute for Education, University of London*

KINGSLEY PRICE *Professor in Philosophy and Education, Johns Hopkins University*

ISRAEL SCHEFFLER *Professor of Education, Graduate School of Education, Harvard University*

EDWARD JOSEPH SHOBEN, JR. *Professor of Education, Teachers College, Columbia University*

FREDERICK A. SIEGLER *Assistant Professor of Philosophy, University of Chicago*

WILSON SMITH *Associate Professor of History and Education, Johns Hopkins University*

J. M. STEPHENS *Professor of Education and Psychology, Johns Hopkins University*

ROBERT M. W. TRAVERS *Professor and Chairman, Department of Educational Psychology, University of Utah*

JOHN WALTON *Professor and Chairman, Department of Education, Johns Hopkins University*

PREFACE

THE CONTRIBUTORS to this volume were asked to address themselves to the question, Is there, or can there be, an academic field or discipline of education? From the results of their inquiry it is apparent that three subsidiary questions arose: What is the nature of an academic discipline? How is the study of education related to the parent disciplines of psychology, history, philosophy, and sociology? and What is the relation between the study of education as professional training and as an academic subject? These three questions provide a convenient order for the presentation of the papers.

Although the authors have attempted to analyze the nature of the formal study of education through consideration of the questions mentioned above, they have in no sense withdrawn from the central problem. The complex subject matter of education and the problems attending its organization have been examined in a variety of ways. The result is a collection of original and scholarly essays on a topic that has been controversial for a long time. Each of the principal essays is followed by a relevant commentary.

There are broader implications. The authors, representing a number of academic disciplines, have quite naturally invoked analogies and made comparisons that reveal the manifold ways in which academic subjects emerge and are organized. Within the peripheral view of this investigation lies the whole of the college curriculum.

Mention should be made of the purpose and setting of the conference that produced these papers. The Department of Education at the Johns Hopkins University occasionally sponsors symposiums on aspects of education in which there is a great deal of current interest but little objective and systematic reflection. This conference met on the campus in May, 1961. It was supported by funds awarded the University for teacher education by the Fund for the Advancement of Education. To the Fund and to the University, which encourages the pursuit of activities of this kind, the participants in this undertaking are extremely grateful.

JOHN WALTON
JAMES L. KUETHE

Baltimore, Maryland
March 14, 1963

CONTENTS

PART ONE

The Nature of a Discipline

I

A Discipline of Education

JOHN WALTON

S ome questions do not admit of a high degree of intellectual rigor in their answers. I am not referring to those questions that, in the words of Immanuel Kant, "transcend every faculty of the mind"; but rather to significant queries and problems for which we can formulate only tentative, imprecise, and approximate solutions. To evade questions of this kind may be admirable in some aspects of academic life, but to limit our formal intellectual activity to those questions that are amenable to rigorous and exact methods of answering is, I think, unwise. At times the prospect of exactness should be balanced by the significance of the question, and by the possibility that imprecise answers may be the first step in the development of more dependable knowledge. The questions which we are asked to consider here—Is there, or can there be, a discipline of Education? and If so, what would it resemble?—seem to me to be questions that can be answered only in a very general and contingent manner. Although I shall attempt to answer them directly, my answers may be only suggestive and programmatic.

Since the discussion which follows anticipates a good many subsidiary questions and is, therefore, somewhat random, a brief outline will be helpful. First, I shall call attention to two general conditions that prevail when scholars convene to engage in an activity of this kind, and that, although not often mentioned, influence the results. Then come the inevitable definitions, after which I attempt to show how a discipline of education may be organized. Following this a number of likely questions are answered, and the discussion closes with a caution or two.

One of the conditions under which all conferences of this kind take place is that the participants are never able to get away from themselves. Each one of us brings to this discussion his own commitments, his own past, and his own biases. The historian, the philosopher, the psychologist, the sociologist, and the educationist arrive here with their own interests and anxieties; and with a vague awareness of the sunken costs in their own scholarship. I, as an educationist, may be more personally involved than the others, since it is my subject that is under scrutiny. And I shall use this rather personal digression to say that this paper is a kind of vehicle of liberation, a resolution of a dilemma, and an opportunity to redeem the study of education from a meretricious professionalism and a slavish dependence on other academic studies.

The second general condition that prevails is the use of language. To say that our thoughts on any subject can be communicated, if not with complete accuracy, then at least with a high degree of mutual understanding, is one of the most significant statements that we can make about the human situation. If we could not make this statement, this paper and this conference on the discipline of education would be pointless. Since we shall exchange our ideas through the medium of language, and since, presumably, we want as accurate a statement of our thoughts as possible—the making of which will in turn enhance the clarity of our thinking—it is necessary that we strive for precision as much as possible in the language we use. Our first responsibility is to define our terms in order to reduce vagueness and ambiguity, not only for the present, but also for the future, in which the recorded expression of our thoughts may be used to influence thought and action, for not only do people communicate through language, they also use recorded language to persuade and influence others.

Proceeding now to the matter of definition, we should first recognize that both "discipline" and "education" have lexical definitions and established usage in the convention of language. Both words are used, separately and together, as a means of communication and have been for a long time, so that certain familiar and public meanings attach themselves to these words. However, both words are sufficiently ambiguous and vague to permit a great deal of unclarity. The temptation is great to resort to purely arbitrary and stipulative definitions. To do so is to incur the risk of adding to the confusion in a realm of thought and language already noteworthy for its lack of clarity. A curious aspect of modern science, and particularly of the social sciences, is the tendency to adopt the Romantic notion of freedom in definition. Irving Babbitt, in his *Rousseau and Romanticism,* remarks on what he calls the irresponsible use of words. A definition, he says, must not reflect our opinion of what a word should mean, but what it actually has meant. Our definitions, therefore, should not only define the words "discipline" and "education" in a more familiar vocabulary (one criterion of a good definition), but they should also observe their lexical and etymological meanings.

By discipline I mean a body of subject matter made up of concepts, facts, and theories, so ordered that it can be deliberately and systematically taught. This definition has a good, if somewhat archaic, lexical foundation. Among the numerous definitions of discipline in the *OED,* we find the following: "a branch of instruction or education; a department of learning or knowledge; a science or art in its educational aspects." It also has a good etymological foundation since discipline and disciple—one who receives instruction—have the same root. A discipline, therefore, is a body of subject matter that is teachable.

By education I mean the whole enterprise of schooling qua schooling, from the nursery school through the university, or any other system of deliberate and organized schooling. This definition, also, is found in the dictionaries which always record historical meanings. To be sure the word education is used in both narrower and broader senses. Henry Adams used it to include practically everything that influenced him throughout his life, the tragic death of his wife being a notable exception; and Bernard Bailyn in his essay entitled "Education in the Forming of American Society" uses it to include all the agencies by which society transmits itself from one generation to another. On the other hand, Alexander Bain, in his *Education as a Science,* would omit from the definition the school as a social institution and limit it to "the means of building up the acquired powers of human beings." Our definition falls between these two extremes. In it education includes the processes of teaching and school learning, the schools as social institutions, and the curriculum as it is related to both.

The question that we are asking at this conference is: Is there, or can there be, a body of systematic knowledge about the phenomena of schooling that resembles other subjects in the curriculum of institutions of higher learning? My answer is: Such a subject exists now only in a most unsatisfactory form; it is, however, not only possible but also highly desirable that it be improved. The empirical subject matter, methods of inquiry, and organized reflections necessary to create such a discipline do exist; it remains only to bring them together and to give them some organization and structure. I shall now proceed to show how I think this organization may be accomplished.

At first glance, the information that is available about education seems to fall into general divisions. The first may be called "the role of the school" and the second, "the process of education." The first includes information about the purposes and goals of organized education, whether they are for the individual, the state, or the *Civitas Dei;* what education has accomplished and what has been said it should accomplish; and its varied and complex relations with other social institutions. The second includes information about human learning, the curriculum, and teaching. This division of subject matter is not new. At present we have courses in the history, philosophy, and sociology of education, and we have courses in teaching, curriculum, and the psychology of learning. Also, others have suggested a similar division. In an inaugural address, delivered at the University of Cambridge in 1928, entitled "The Study of Political Science," Sir Ernest Barker said:

> The theory of education is essentially a part of political theory. It is not so much a matter of psychology, with which it has been generally connected in the Universities and Training Colleges where it is taught (though I admit that the study of psychology has a value for the theory of education, as it has for political theory in general): it is rather a matter of social theory—of grasping and comprehending the purposes, the character, and the needs of Society and the State, and of discovering the methods by which the young can best be trained to achieve these purposes, to maintain and even improve that character, and to satisfy those needs.[1]

I am proposing that "the school as a social institution" and "the process of education" be used as two very general categories for the classification of the subject matter of education. Certainly the two are related and the discipline of education will comprise the study of these relations; but for the present, I should like to see how much of the information that exists about education can be organized around these two general ideas.

I shall now go into some detail about procedures that may be used to develop a discipline of education. Let us take first the division "the role of the school." The first step is the collection of the information about the school as a social institution that now reposes in the disciplines of philosophy, history, law, sociology, anthropology, and political science, and education. Traditional philosophy and educational philosophy have a substantial literature on the subject. To this we should add the historical information which is even more voluminous. One has only to look at the references in Bernard Bailyn's essay "Education in the Forming of American Society" to see how much work has been done on American education alone; and a vast amount of scattered information is imbedded in the volumes of general history, both documentary and interpretative.

1. *Church, State and Education,* Ann Arbor Paperbacks (Ann Arbor: University of Michigan, 1957), p. 192.

So far I have suggested the mere collecting and compiling of the information and ideas about the role of organized education that are now included in the subject matter of philosophy and history. This task, even with the aid of modern methods of collecting, classifying, and indexing, would be extremely tedious. But there certainly would be opportunities all along for tentative organization of the subject matter, for theorizing, the investigation of original sources, and the discovery of new knowledge. For example, after the series of observations below one might arrive at an interesting hypothesis. When Athens fell in 404 B.C. at the close of the Peloponnesian War, the political and social crisis greatly increased the stress on education and enhanced its importance. In the 1630's and 40's when the New England Puritans faced the implacable wilderness, they made extraordinary corporate efforts to establish educational institutions. In 1806, after the Napoleonic wars, the German nation followed the urgent advice of Fichte and became intense about education as a means to national preeminence. And immediately after the Russians thrust Sputnik into orbit, the United States began massive programs for educational reform in and through the schools. If we look for common circumstances in these events, we observe at least two: first, there exists a society in a high state of civilization, and, second, conditions exist which threaten a perceptible corrosion or the immediate destruction of its dominant values, or even its very existence. That the importance of education in society increases when these two conditions prevail is an interesting and plausible hypothesis.

The subject matter on the role of the school may be gathered also from the social sciences—from anthropology, sociology, and political science. In sociology and anthropolgy we find education a major concern. For example, Karl Mannheim sees an expansion of the role of formal education in modern society: "The modern school has no choice but to intensify and broaden its contacts with other areas of life and social institutions; it will have to give up its older, purely scholastic character, the more it takes over functions neglected by other social institutions." [2] Also, in political science and government one finds rather clear notions about the subject. In the legal literature of the United States, and particularly in the case law, there are many judicial opinions and obiter dicta that provide some evidence of what the role of education has been.

These extremely brief suggestions are illustrative of the sources and kinds of subject matter that are available. Although we may collect a substantial body of fact and opinion, it will undoubtedly be fragmentary, contradictory, and archipelagic. Certainly, the mere compilation of this information would not meet our requirements for a body of subject matter so ordered that it can be taught. But this is only the first step. The second is an attempt to bring some kind of order into the chaos.

I have already indicated how, during the collection of the subject matter, patterns of organization, varied and tentative structures, and plausible theories of middle and lower ranges may suggest themselves. Prolonged scrutiny of and reflection on the material will certainly yield chronological and logical arrangements that will provide the means for organization. Furthermore, it will provide the opportunity for the systematic extension of the knowledge we have. We can hardly hope for a master scheme of organization, for a vast, architectonic theory that would unify all the disparate information gathered from a variety of sources, but we may expect theories of the middle range, rival theories, working hypotheses, comparative data, and a very general framework into which they all may fit more or less comfortably, although there will always be what Talcott Parsons calls the "residual categories." We may have chronological and comparative arrangements of what the role of the school is and has been; we may have a body of scientific knowledge about what the school can do under a variety

2. *Freedom, Power and Democratic Planning* (New York: Oxford University Press, 1950), pp. 248–49.

of conditions, and we may have a rather elegant arrangement for the great theories about what organized education should be and do.

Up to this point I have discussed, very briefly to be sure, how I think the information and ideas that we already have about the role of the school may be collected and organized; and according to the definitions at the beginning of this paper, if what I have suggested can be accomplished for both the role of the school and the educational process, we can have a discipline of education. The importance of this activity should not be minimized; the sheer compilation of information is a service to scholarship, and the reorganization of existing knowledge is often scholarship of the highest form. But it would be highly desirable and fashionable if our discipline of education could be so organized that it could not only be taught, but that it would also be a means and a stimulation to the discovery of new knowledge. The existing methods of investigation and inquiry are available to it as they are to all disciplines.

The information and theories that are available about "the process of education," the more scientific and, perhaps, the more useful of our two divisions of the discipline, should be collected and organized in a manner similar to the one described above. Here serious study and reflection should again yield structures for the organization of our present knowledge, and theories that will be productive of testable hypotheses and the discovery of new knowledge. A great deal of this sort of thing has already been done; I should like to see it continued. In this area of our discipline we shall be dealing with teaching, learning, and the curriculum in their complicated relations. The nature and conditions of human learning, the logic and structure of disciplines, and the commonplace but mysterious art of teaching must all be seen as a part of the educational process. Perhaps we shall find greater gaps and discontinuities than we anticipate; perhaps learning is always at odds with teaching; perhaps, when a student is *in statu pupillari,* he must follow and accept the settled orders of knowledge, whether those orders are correct or not, or whether or not the logic of organized knowledge is consonant with the psychology of learning. But these are questions for the scholars of education and questions which I think are as exciting as those presented by other disciplines. Also, these scholars of education, as they take an unhurried view of their subject, will undoubtedly perceive relations between our two general divisions of educational knowledge, and new orders of knowledge will ensue.

Having indicated very briefly the initial steps in the organization of a discipline of education, I shall try to anticipate and to answer some of the questions and objections that may arise. First, someone may attempt to impose the test of uniqueness on the subject matter I have suggested. The question is often asked when this matter of a discipline of education is discussed, What is the unique subject matter of education? Let us admit that any discipline or subject of study should concern itself with a body of subject matter that is not included, or treated in the same way, in another discipline. Otherwise, there would be differentiation in name only. Now it is obvious that many of the phenomena of education, as we have defined it, are unique, despite the once popular cliché that education is life. Who can mistake a classroom for anything else? What does a curriculum resemble? Even college campuses are easily recognizable; and a great many people say that they are able to identify a college professor on sight. Perhaps only educational administrators lack academic distinction, or should I say distinctiveness? But we may all agree that education, as we have defined it, is a distinct phenomenon and still argue that it is not, or cannot be, the subject of a respectable academic discipline because (1) we know very little about it, (2) it lacks a system of organization and methods of inquiry, or (3) it is adequately studied in other disciplines. I shall comment briefly on these three reservations.

First, it is difficult to say how much systematic knowledge is available about education, since this knowledge is widely scattered among other disciplines. If we were to collect, cull, and organize this information, we would have at least a modest body of subject matter.

Second, we need not look for any unique system of organization —although we may find one—nor need we possess unique methods for the extension of knowledge. How many of the subjects now taught in colleges and universities would qualify as disciplines if they were required to have a unique organization and method of extension? Logic, perhaps, but then logic is dependent to some extent on language. Mathematics, considered as one of the purest disciplines, borrows from logic; and all the sciences borrow from mathematics. Perhaps history with its chronology comes nearest to being the one discipline that has a unique system. The other social sciences employ a variety of methods of organization and inquiry and hold a monopoly on none.

Finally, the fact that the subject matter of education is now widely dispersed is no argument that it should remain so. We may have a Diaspora in reverse; and we have already passed beyond the bounds of the law of parsimony in the introduction of new disciplines. We have already begun the creation of a new discipline. We may now appropriate from psychology the information about school learning; from history, the body of knowledge about the purposes of education; from philosophy, the methods of dealing with values; and from the social sciences, the fragmentary material they have about the social and political relations of education. We may reasonably ask, What is the justification for keeping the subject matter of education dispersed except that now it enlarges the boundaries of other empires? The discipline of political science includes the study of political theory, political behavior, and political organization. Why should the study of education not include theories and information about teaching and learning, and about the educational organization? Moreover, we may add to these aspects of education not now included in other disciplines, such as teaching, curriculum, and the role of the school. Of course nearly everyone talks about these matters, but there is little systematic study of them. If the argument is advanced that the study of education should be restricted to these neglected aspects, I should like to ask why they should be studied in isolation from the inquiry about learning, about the historical development of education, and about its theoretical foundations.

Another question that may arise is, Why study the phenomena of education in the context of the school? Or, in other words, Why use an institution as the basis for the organization of a discipline? This leads us into one of the most complicated of all academic problems—the basis for the differentiation of subject matter. A casual observation reveals that academic disciplines have a variety of modes of differentiation and organization, and that these modes came about for a variety of reasons. For example, within the discipline of history we may subdivide and differentiate the subject matter rather neatly by centuries, epochs, or civilizations. Or we may organize our knowledge of the past around an aspect of civilization such as art, science, or economics. In sociology, the phenomena of social life, its organization, relations, and behavior provide the basis for a discipline; while in political science one form of social organization and activity, that of government, comprises the whole discipline, and it is studied historically, empirically, and theoretically. In psychology certain aspects of human behavior, such as learning, are studied whenever they occur in living organisms. In biophysics and social psychology, related phenomena from different disciplines are combined to form a new discipline. In literature the language in which the literature is written sets the broadest limits of the discipline, although we may have comparative literature. And in oceanography our lines of demarcation are coterminous with coast lines. Some disciplines deal only with special skills and techniques, for example, logic and statistics.

We should note also that there is considerable overlapping among these various disciplines. Both biology and oceanography include the study of marine life; both philosophy and political science include political theory; both Latin and history include Roman civilization; and sociology, psychology, and political science all concern themselves with voting behavior. It would be most unusual if many of the phenomena included in our discipline of education were not also included in other disciplines. Learning in rats, pigeons, chimpanzees, and men will continue to be a part of the discipline of psychology, but learning under the special conditions of boy, book, and teacher should be the special concern of education. Furthermore, school learning should be studied in close relation to the purposes and goals of organized education.

I still have not justified the selection of an institution—in this case the school—as a basis for a division of knowledge. There are, I think, two good reasons for this focus or center for a discipline. The first is simple: organized education is a historic, discrete, complex, and important activity in which many people, and most people concerned with scholarship, are interested. Furthermore, knowledge about education will be increased if the study of it is designed to increase our knowledge about education rather than about some other field. I have a strong impression that knowledge in the sciences has advanced through an interest in and the study of a specific area of phenomena. The second reason is more complicated: in the systematic study of education we are compelled to deal with different kinds of phenomena and to employ a variety of methods of research and inquiry. On the one hand, we are inevitably concerned with what may be referred to as a science, the science of education at whatever stage of progress it finds itself. Consequently, we shall be dealing with quantitative measurements, predictability, probability, precise degrees of relationship, and the whole legacy of positivism. On the other hand, we shall be forced to deal with values and with the existential aspects of education, with quality and uniqueness, with the arts and history. In the discipline of education, C. P. Snow's two cultures will stand side by side: it will be both a scientific and a humanistic discipline. Since all rationalism tends toward monism, there will undoubtedly be attempts at synthesis. In the foreseeable future, we can expect only that the two aspects of our discipline will be viewed in close association, and that they may be seen as complementary; but in time we may develop a language of education that will enable us to converse intelligently about the enterprise as a whole.

Now if the phenomena of education are so discrete, complex, and related to one another that they readily provide a valid and sufficient content for an academic discipline, and if there are no copyrights on methods of organization and inquiry—if observation, conceptualization, classification, analysis, theorizing, and experimentation; if logic, originality, imagination, and curiosity are public domain—why have we not developed a respectable academic discipline of education? There are, I think, three reasons. First, we have consumed our energies in professional training programs or in the solution of practical and urgent problems (this statement does not apply to a great many of the first generation of educationists). Second, there has been a maidenly reluctance—to understate the matter—on the part of well-established disciplines to encourage such a development. For some of them it might mean relinquishing part of their subject matter; and, for all of them, it would mean admitting into their midst a discipline that might be disquieting. And third, in the study of education we are confronted with what looks like the first step in an infinite regression: the systematic study and teaching of a great variety of subjects would itself become the subject of study (as a matter of fact, in this conference we are studying the study of study).

Another question, or series of questions, has undoubtedly arisen by this time about the relations of the discipline of education that has been described to practice and to research. The relationship to the former is complicated and unclear. I have dealt with it at some length in an article entitled "The Study and Practice of Teaching";[3] but I have done no more than to suggest that there is an inevitable gap between systematic study and practice due to the different conditions under which each occurs. What appears to be a rather close relationship may really be an illusion, the pursuit of which may be hazardous to both the development of a discipline

3. *School Review*, LXIX, No. 2 (Autumn, 1961), 136–50.

and to sound practice. The fact that the study of education can apparently be related to an important practical activity may be used to justify an inadequate and poorly organized discipline; and any academic discipline, however well developed, may be used to despoil sound and effective practice. That the discipline of education will be useful for practice cannot be doubted, but I do not propose here to go into the problem of relationship.

The relationship to research seems to me to be much simpler. Merely collecting and organizing the information about education that is available would be a contribution to knowledge. Furthermore, the new discipline would not only reveal the gaps in our knowledge but it would also suggest lines of thought and investigation that may be extremely fruitful for an increase of our knowledge about all aspects of schooling. And the results of our inquiry would be fed back into the body of knowledge about education.

In attempting to show how a discipline of education may be organized, and at the same time stressing the importance of such study, I have a number of reservations and cautionary concerns. Education, like many other social sciences, is subject to the great temptation—the temptation of power over the affairs of men. I fear the urgency and importance of education. It is a region that contains questions, the answers to which matter a great deal to happiness, progress, and even survival. Without a sound and well-organized body of knowledge, and without rigorous methods of inquiry, we may succumb to the temptation of developing a spurious discipline. If this happens, the judgment will be the same in the future as it is now: "Ridiculous, the waste, sad time stretching before and after." If, on the other hand, we are willing to take what looks like a retrograde step and begin the slow, disinterested study of the phenomena of education, we may develop sooner than we expect an important social science that will have interest for the serious scholar and long-range practical consequences for society. Between this idea of a discipline of education and the reality fall two shadows. They are the shadows of impatience and indolence. The former is much the darker of the two.

COMMENTS   *R. S. Peters*

I have two main points to make, one of them negative and the other positive, about the conception of "A Discipline of Education" as set out by Mr. Walton.

To begin with the negative point: I just cannot grasp the thesis that education could ever be *a* discipline in any ordinary sense; it is rather a focus or a meeting place of disciplines. To start with, I think that the notion that disciplines have subject matters is an archaic relic of the old Baconian myth about scientific method. It may make some sort of sense if one is trying to distinguish sciences at a low level of theoretical development from each other. For instance, one might distinguish ornithology from petrology by reference to their subject matter. But what is the subject matter of physics or chemistry? The notion of a subject matter might have some practical value for the fixing of a syllabus, the setting of examinations, and the organization of university departments. But its importance extends little beyond this level. How, for instance, would one distinguish psychology from anthropology or from sociology by reference to subject matter? Presumably they are all concerned with the study of man. The point is that they ask and try to answer quite different types of questions about man. Sciences can only be vaguely distinguished from each other by reference to the types of questions that they ask and the types of answers which they give and by the types of procedure which they employ in testing such answers.

Historically speaking, what happens is that questions arise and some kind of systematic attempt is made to answer them. A discipline develops when there are some reasonably well-worked-out and structured answers to such questions which come to form a body of knowledge, together with techniques and procedures for developing better answers or for dealing with new problems which these answers give rise to. A discipline, as Mr. Walton says, is a body of knowledge that is teachable. But this involves a mastery of procedures for testing answers to certain types of questions as well as a body of knowledge. A good disciple is one who can eventually dispense with his teacher. For he will have mastered the procedures of the discipline which permit him to manage on his own.

These various disciplines are concerned with quite different sorts of questions, and if the case of education is considered it is absurd to think that the various disciplines that have bearing on education could ever be coordinated into one discipline. I will indicate one obvious and another not so obvious illustration of this point. Mr. Walton mentions philosophy as well as sociology as being concerned with the role of the school, with its purposes and goals. But the philosopher is not concerned in at all the same kind of way as the sociologist is with such matters. The sociologist tries to describe, for instance, the job done by the school in a society, and to theorize about how its goals are related to more general social valuations. But the philosopher is concerned with what it *means* for a school to have a goal, purpose, or function and with what sort of justification can be given for the goal suggested. He is concerned with conceptual analysis, with patterns of argument, and with criteria of justification; he is not concerned with description and explanation as is the sociologist. And just as the sociologist must have an intensive training in assessing evidence and in statistical techniques if he is going to answer his types of question in a disciplined way, so also the philosopher must have a very rigorous training of a quite different sort if he is to talk about such matters in a manner which rises above "Lift Up Your Hearts," Channel 2 style. He must be thoroughly trained in epistemology, philosophy of mind, ethics, and social philosophy. To train people in even two such disciplines at once is quite an undertaking. I have experience of this; for my job at the University of London is to train people for the joint degree in Philosophy and Psychology, which involves at least a three-year course in the central problems of both these disciplines. Even these closely linked disciplines are concerned with such dif-

ferent types of problem and employ such different types of procedure for answering them that only very able students can gain
some sort of mastery of both these disciplines. Yet what other disciplines are more central to education than these? To contemplate
subsuming, not just these two disciplines, but also history and
sociology under a general discipline of education not only seems
to me logically absurd; it is also, I should say, practically impossible.

Furthermore, even if one leaves out philosophy and history, and
considers simply the theoretical sciences of sociology and psychology, here again there is not, and never could be a discipline; there
are a number of disciplines. The notion that theories and concepts
might be developed to cover the role of the school and the process
of education is to assume that it might be possible to develop
unifying theories in the sciences of man such as one finds in physics
and mechanics. I think that this whole approach to the social
sciences is fundamentally mistaken. Indeed even within psychology
there are different types of questions to answer which subordinate
disciplines are developing, let alone within the social sciences generally. I have argued elsewhere that, even if the limited field of
motivation [4] within psychology is considered, it is impossible to
develop any sort of unifying theory to answer all the different ways
of taking the question, Why did X do Y? To think of *a* discipline
of education, which will include not only psychology and the other
social sciences, but also history and philosophy as well, seems to
me to ignore all sorts of crucial distinctions for the sake of a cause.

But enough of my negative criticism. My positive suggestion is
that though education could never be a discipline, an approach to
education which draws more on the established disciplines would
not only benefit education but would also benefit the disciplines
themselves. The first part of this thesis is so obvious that it scarcely
needs elaborating. To take examples from my own field: I am
appalled by the looseness, fogginess, and general lack of rigour
that one meets when reading some of the literature on issues such

4. *The Concept of Motivation* (London: Kegan Paul, 1958).

as "democracy in education," where the educator derives his "authority" from, "equality of opportunity" in education, and the "aims of education." It is no wonder that most philosophers regard this field as a philosophical slum. But it need not be so. There are genuine and exciting philosophical problems in this field. Indeed there is enough work to keep a company of trained philosophers busy for half a century. And such work could contribute much to the clear-headedness of teachers on the job.

I will illustrate the second part of my positive thesis, that the disciplines themselves could profit by contact with problems of education, by reference to psychology and philosophy, which are the two disciplines with which I am familiar. The philosophy of education is, roughly speaking, a meeting place for epistemology, philosophy of mind, ethics, and social philosophy. I find that taking the concrete situation of the teacher in a school system is often an admirable way of trying out conceptual analyses and theories of justification and bringing them down to earth. Often philosophers construct imaginary examples to test out their analyses and arguments. But it is very easy to rig these to fit the theory. If one is considering matters to do with equality, toleration, punishment, authority, the training of character and emotions, the difference between conditioning, indoctrinating, and teaching, and so on (all of which exemplify general philosophical problems), the concrete example of the school situation is very valuable. I have learned much, for instance, about the difficulties of developing arguments to justify the "intrinsically good" activities of the Ideal Utilitarians from teachers, whose main job is to pass on such activities to children who are very often in the position of Mill's pig. The philosophy clarifies the teacher's position, and the concrete arguments emerging, as it were, from the trenches of the educational battlefield do much to test out the philosophical theories. This two-way flow from practical concerns to philosophical analysis and back again into teaching should be a continuing source of material enrichment.

Similarly in psychology. I have elsewhere argued: "Far from it being the case that educationists have a lot to learn from the theory of learning, I want to suggest that the psychology of learning could benefit enormously from a study of the practice of education. . . . On the one hand learning theory might benefit enormously by the careful experimental study of situations under which human beings learn all sorts of different things rather than by concentration on highly artificial situations where rats and dogs learn very limited things. On the other hand generalizations developed by psychologists might really be of some use to teachers and other practical people who have the function of passing on the skills and knowledge essential to civilization. Indeed the psychology of learning might even cease to be an embarrassment to distraught lecturers who have the thankless task of trying to teach aspiring teachers how to teach." [5]

There is the further positive point, too, that education provides a very fruitful field where workers in the different disciplines can meet. A center of interest such as this can do much to develop understanding of other disciplines and the cross-fertilization which is so often advocated as being so beneficial in an era of increasing specialization. My own interest, for instance, in education derives both from my practical experience as a schoolmaster and from the fact that, theoretically speaking, I am a borderline man. (My present interest is in the borderline Scheer psychology and ethics.) To deal with problems connected with character, emotions, mental health, and moral education, a training in both philosophy and psychology is essential; for they are difficult to tackle clearheadedly unless conceptual analysis is combined with empirical research.

Two disciplines are here relevant; but a common focus of interest does not make of them *one* discipline.

My thesis, then, in a nutshell, is that there can never be *a* discipline of education. But a more disciplined approach to the problems of education could be of great benefit both to education and

5. *Authority, Responsibility and Education* (London: Allen and Unwin, 1960), p. 137.

to the disciplines which deal systematically with the various types of theoretical problems to which this practical activity gives rise. Education, like medicine, is a profession, not a discipline. But it can only be an effective one if it draws on the disciplines which lean on its problems.

II

Discipline in Teaching
In Its Study and in Its Theory

KINGSLEY PRICE

In one of its employments, the word "education" marks out activities of teaching. Although we call them by a single phrase, these activities are, in fact, widely diverse. The teachers of swimming, of painting, of piano, of the English language, of morals, of Roman history, of chemistry, of arithmetic—all these teach something to their students. But what each of them promises and the procedures by which he hopes to accomplish it is different. The abilities to swim, to paint, to perform on the piano, to speak English, to act rightly are abilities to do radically different things; yet each of them is proffered as the successful outcome of some teaching activity. Knowing the career of Rome, the structures of atoms, and the relations of numbers—all, again, concern themselves with objects which are very unlike; yet each is a possession of those whose instruction in these subjects is successful. Moreover, the procedures by which teachers strive to establish in their students a mastery of their subjects are highly varied. Working with students in the pool, at the easel, at the keyboard; explaining the use of words; discussing different alternatives in a moral situation, the transition from Republic to Empire; supervising chemical experiments; showing what it is to count and add—it is hard to imagine human activities more radically remote from each other than these.

Still, if we look at education only in this way, we fail to notice a certain important similarity in its activities. All those we have mentioned are directed toward a goal, the student's mastery of some subject; and we would not call anything a "teaching activity" which lacked direction toward the acquisition of something—some skill, attitude, or knowledge. Different teaching activities possess this feature in different degrees. It is present to a high degree in formal teaching situations. When the arithmetic teacher announces, "Today we are going to learn the multiplication table for two," his activity possesses a goal to a high degree. But when, from a rambling conversation about Plato, a student emerges with an interpretation of Plato's views on justice, we realize that his acquiring it may have been only dimly present as a goal in the conversation. While the goal of mastery may be present in different degrees, there can be no teaching activity which lacks it altogether. Such an activity would be a teaching of nothing at all; and that, in the language of the schools, is a logical absurdity. The goals of education are enormously varied; but direction toward some goal, dim or clear, characterizes all of it.

There is a second similarity present in all teaching activities. This is the knowledge of rules for the attainment of the goal. To teach the Australian crawl, let the student practice the arm stroke and the breathing on dry land first; to establish control at the keyboard, bring the student to feel that he plays from the shoulder and on the bottom of the keys; to foster generosity and kindliness, show the student some of the sorrows of mankind and their origin in mean and thoughtless motives; to bring about an understanding of Rome, point to similarities with familiar features of present day life—these typify the rules for teaching activities. Such rules are not always present to the teacher in the same way. Sometimes they lurk in the background and are known to him in the way we all know the rules of our mother tongue, without thought or care. At other times, they stand in the foreground and are attended to in the way a young and worried piano teacher regards the rules precipitated out of his own tutelage, deliberately and with concern to employ those that are useful. It may be implicit or it may be explicit; but the teacher's knowledge of rules for achieving mastery of his subject is requisite to his teaching activity. Where that knowledge is clearly wanting, there may be baby sitting, protective custody, or any number of things; but no teaching. Teaching requires the knowledge of rules for the achievement of its goals.

But this knowledge of rules is not enough. We can imagine a person who knows all the rules for teaching swimming, generosity, and arithmetic; but who, nonetheless, teaches no one to master these subjects. Such a person would be a scholar of the teaching of swimming, morals, and arithmetic; but he would not be a teacher of them. The reason is that he does not try to employ the rules as guides to the achievement of mastery. He must intend to make use of the rules to realize the goals of instruction; and in this way his intention includes the first two features we have described. Teaching consists in an activity which expresses the intention to use rules as guides to the mastery of some subject. Anyone who engages in activity of this kind, engages in education.[1]

While the intention to use the rules as guides to a goal is enough to make an activity one of teaching, it does not guarantee the success of that activity. Suppose there are several persons, all of whom try to employ rules for bringing about a mastery of the technique of piano performance. Suppose, further, that the rules are adequate to the goal. They are all teachers; but we can imagine that some should fail completely, while others should succeed to some degree. The reason is that some do not see at all how to apply the rules, while others see it with varying degrees of clarity. All try to employ the rule about playing from the shoulder. But some do not at

1. This first use of the word "education" does not mark off a range of activities by a sharp line. Each teaching activity intentionally uses rules to establish a goal; but since the intention, the rules, and the goal may be more or less clearly present, it shades off gradually into something different. Teaching activities are surrounded by others of which it would be hard to say, without a deliberate decision, that they are or are not teaching activities. Consider the mother's spontaneous training of the infant, or our own spontaneous correction of newcomers learning our language.

all see how to bring just this student to play that way, while others
see it more or less plainly. The first have no ability to apply the
rules; they do not succeed at all. The others succeed in varying
degrees. The teacher's ability to apply the rules in concrete cases
is a condition for his success.[2] Education is a name for all those
activities which express the intention to employ rules to realize
mastery of some subject; while successful education marks out
among them those activities which also embody some ability, varying in the success of its exercise, to see how to apply the rules in
particular cases.

Is education, in this first sense of the word, a discipline? Let us
consider some activities which are undoubted disciplines. Consider, first, the life of the monastery. Here, the day is blocked out
in segments of time, to each of which some activity is assigned—
devotion to some, work to others, eating to still others, and so on.
The purpose of this regulation is the achievement of beatitude; it
is in the hope of finding blessedness that the member follows the
rules of the order. But the day of the worldling is either not made up
of times whose activities are prescribed; or if this should be the
case, the prescription is not directed toward achieving some single
goal. He acts upon caprice, not upon rule; or if upon rule such as
that of money-making, only in order to satisfy his caprices as they
appear from time to time. Consider, also, the life of the soldier.
Each part of his day, like the day of the monk, is devoted to a
prescribed activity—to marching, to eating, to recreation in favorable circumstances—all this in order to accomplish a single purpose, that of an army in high readiness. But the vagabond suffers
from no such fatal necessity. He does what he likes when he likes,
moving to his advantage with the calendar, limited by nothing but
the availability of trailer camps. These differences between the
monk and the worldling, the soldier and the vagabond, come to
this: that the monk and the soldier deliberately accept a regimen
in order to secure a goal, while the worldling and the vagabond ac-

2. Of course, it may not be enough since, in addition to the teacher's
ability, other factors may be involved in mastery.

cept no such regimen, or no such goal. The former lead lives which are disciplines; the latter do not. A discipline, we may say, is a human activity characterized by following *rules* in order to achieve a goal.

We can see, now, that every teaching activity is very much like a discipline in this respect. The teacher of arithmetic employs rules in order that his student should secure mastery of that subject as the monk adopts a regimen in order to achieve beatitude and the soldier, in order to maintain military readiness. The monk and the soldier follow rules which prescribe more of their lives than most teachers; the religious and the military interests command more of one's time than does the activity of teaching. Still, when one is engaged in teaching, his life is subject to rules for securing goals as are those governed by the monastery and the army. And it is not wrong to describe education as a discipline.

But it is not quite right either. The life of the monk is a single discipline; it is dominated by a single goal and informed by a single regimen. So, also, is that of the soldier. But while all education, like these lives, involves the intentional employment of rules for the achievement of goals, its regimens and goals are, as we have seen, enormously varied. Teaching people how to swim and self-reliance in the water is a very different thing from teaching people how to add and the knowledge of arithmetic, however much each involves following rules toward a goal. The teaching of swimming, of painting, of piano, of the English language, of morals, of history, of chemistry, and of arithmetic are not one single discipline; and education is a great many disciplines, as many as there are kinds of teaching activities. Where "education" stands for these activities, we must answer the question for this conference by saying that education is not *a* discipline, but many disciplines together.

There is a second employment of the word "education," closely allied with the first. It is the use given to it in one part of most university catalogues, the part devoted to courses in education. Here, frequently its role is to stand not for teaching activities (one hopes that such courses do not exclude them), but for the study of those activities, for research into them. What question might the study of teaching activities answer? They are disciplines as we have seen, and the question which is paramount for the study of disciplines concerns the conditions for their excellence. Each teaching activity is the intentional employment of rules for the establishment of mastery in its subject, and each successful teaching activity is the successful exercise of the teacher's ability to see how to apply the rules in his concrete situation—the actual securing of mastery to some degree in some subject through application of rules. But the excellence of his discipline is another matter. The teacher's success is determined by the utility of rules employed and by his ability to see how to apply them. But we may ask whether the mastery his success assures is a good thing, whether the entire activity of trying to secure it is worthwhile. The moral nature of the goal and of the discipline of achieving it, the excellence of the entire discipline, includes its success; for an activity could not be morally excellent which never succeeded to any degree. But the excellence of a discipline is different from its success; for a discipline we describe as excellent is one the moral nature of whose goal suffuses the entire discipline, painting the neutrality of mere success with the more splendid colors of virtue. Education, in the second sense of the word, is the effort to discover the conditions for the utility of rules, and the conditions for the ability to apply them —the conditions for the success of teaching activities. But it is also the effort to discover conditions for the excellence of those activities. It is the study of the conditions for excellence of education in the first sense. We must now explain this view.

What kind of statements are the rules which teachers employ? We might suppose that they are statements which tell the teacher all the things he must do to the student in order that the latter should achieve mastery of the subject. Let us represent mastery of the subject by B; and all the things which must be done to achieve it, by A, C, D, and E. We might suppose, then, that a teaching rule is any statement of the form, "To establish B, simply introduce A, C, D, and E." It is clear that we could formulate no rule of this form unless we knew to be true some statement which had the form, "A, C, D, and E always accompany B, and nothing else relevant ever accompanies B." A true statement of this form would set forth the necessary and sufficient conditions for B, and a rule for teaching B could be derived from it by changing the position of its components and altering their mood. A rule for teaching, we might suppose, is a statement which tells us how to establish mastery of some subject, and which is derived in the way indicated from a true statement of the necessary and sufficient conditions for that mastery.

The difficulty with this view is that we cannot know what rules are rules of the form described. We cannot know to be true any statement which sets forth the necessary and sufficient conditions for B; consequently, we cannot know what rule makes use of them. If we knew it to be true, for example, that the shoulder feeling, interest in proficient performance, freedom from the score, and a liking for music always accompany mastery of technique, while nothing else relevant ever accompanies it, we could state the rule, "To establish technique, bring the student to have the shoulder feeling, interest in proficiency, freedom from the score, and liking for music." But we cannot know that these are the necessary and sufficient conditions for mastery. A, C, D, and E might always accompany B so far as our observation extends; but elsewhere, B might turn up without one or more of them. If we require that a teaching rule for B set forth its necessary and sufficient conditions, we can never recognize such a rule, for we can never know what values take the place of the variables A, C, D, and E. Perhaps at the end of time, someone will state the necessary and sufficient conditions for B; but that statement will not enable us to recognize a rule for teaching B since it will be too late to change the position of its components and alter their mood—too late, indeed, for teaching B at all.[3]

Let us make another try. We might suppose that a rule tells the teacher at least one thing he must do to the student in order that he should achieve mastery. Such a rule would be a statement of the form, "To establish B, always introduce A"; it could not be formulated unless we knew some statement to be true which had the form, "Wherever B occurs, A occurs." Such a statement would set forth a necessary condition for B, and a rule for teaching B could be derived from it by altering the mood of its components.

Again the difficulty is that we cannot recognize any concrete rules to be of this kind. A statement of the form, "B always accompanies A" cannot be known to be true. However often proficient technique and the shoulder feeling march together in our observation, they may be separated elsewhere. We cannot, therefore, recognize any one thing as one which must be done in order to achieve proficiency; nor any concrete rule as possessing the form, "To establish B, always introduce A." [4]

A rule for teaching B is of the form, "To establish B, introduce A." Such a rule can be formulated by reference to a statement of the form, "A sometimes accompanies B." Such a statement sets forth neither necessary nor sufficient conditions for B. But since it states what does sometimes accompany B, it enables us to derive a rule from it by changing the position of its components and altering their mood. Unlike those just considered, this statement does

3. It is difficult to see how a statement of the necessary and sufficient conditions for B can be regarded as probable, and as yielding a probable rule for teaching B. A precise determination of its probability would be phrased in terms of the number of times A, C, D, and E accompany B out of a total number of occurrences of B; and this admits of the absence of A, C, D, or E from B in some cases. But this absence is incompatible with the notion of necessary and sufficient conditions for B.

4. It does not help to hold that the statement of a necessary condition for B might be known to be probable. For to hold that A is probably a necessary condition for B is compatible with instances in which A and B do not accompany each other; and these instances are incompatible with the proposition that B always accompanies A.

provide a concrete value for A, and consequently, a concrete rule of the form, "To establish B, introduce A."

Consider the rule, "To establish mastery at the keyboard, bring the student to have the shoulder feeling." This rule can be derived from the statement that the shoulder feeling sometimes accompanies mastery at the keyboard. This statement makes no claim to necessary or sufficient conditions for that mastery, but it does yield a rule for teaching it. Consider also the rule, "To establish an understanding of other times, point out their similarities to familiar aspects of the student's own culture." This rule corresponds to the statement, "Seeing their similarities to familiar aspects of his own culture, on some occasions, promotes the student's understanding of other times." This statement makes no grand claim about the conditions for historical understanding, but it does yield a rule for teaching it. A teaching rule is a statement of the form, "To establish B, introduce A," which is secured in the way indicated from a statement of the form, "A sometimes accompanies B." A teaching statement is any statement thus related to a teaching rule.

What are the conditions for the utility of employing a teaching rule? The first is that its teaching statement should be known to be true. If we did not know it to be true that the shoulder feeling sometimes accompanies proficiency, employing the teaching rule it yields would be as useless as employing any that we might merely imagine; and teaching piano technique could not be distinguished from pretending to teach it. Like considerations apply to the conditions for the utility of employing rules to establish the mastery of morals, history, and arithmetic. A teaching rule is a useful one if its teaching statement is known to be true.[5]

This first condition for the utility of employing rules does not guarantee success in teaching. A teaching statement does not set

5. It is possible that the utility of some teaching rules should consist in their possessing teaching statements which are known to be probable, but not known to be true. Such statements might be rendered probable by the evidence, but not shown to be true by observation of the things to which they refer. Such a condition would make it useful to employ the teaching rules derivable from them.

forth all the occurrences which accompany mastery, nor even one that is necessary for it. The shoulder feeling, interest in proficiency, and a liking for music may not be enough for mastery; each of them might be lacking where it is found. Even so, if it is true that they sometimes accompany mastery, there is some probability that using one or all of the rules based upon the statements of them will make for it. In this sense, we should understand the utility of the first condition for those rules.[6]

There is a second condition for the utility of teaching rules. Teaching statements are true only in certain circumstances. Consider the teaching statement that the shoulder feeling sometimes accompanies mastery at the keyboard. For the cases in which this statement is true, it must also be true that the persons who possess mastery have normal hands and arms, pianos, time to practice, and many other things which cannot be listed. Similarly, those cases in which it is true that noticing their similarities to one's own culture furthers the understanding of other times must also be cases in which the student is sufficiently interested in his own culture to notice its constituents, is aware of the past, knows how to reckon time, and so forth. The truth of any teaching statement presupposes circumstances which the statement, itself, does not describe.[7]

6. I do not account, here, for the possibility that some such teaching rules might be incompatible in their application. The situation might be formulated as follows: "C sometimes accompanies B," and "Not-C sometimes accompanies B." Teaching statements of these forms would be conditions, respectively, for the utility of teaching rules of the forms: "To establish B, introduce C" and "To establish B, prevent C." In such cases, the more useful rule to follow is the one whose teaching statement is better supported; but in a particular case, one might be obliged to resort to the rule whose teaching statement is less well supported. This resort is familiar to all teachers.

7. There is no sharp distinction between a teaching statement and a statement of some circumstance which the former presupposes. They look very much alike: "The shoulder feeling sometimes accompanies mastery"; "Interest in music sometimes accompanies mastery"; "Normal hands and arms sometimes accompany mastery." The first of these is clearly a teaching statement, the second one a little less so, and the third one not at all in ordinary situations. We derive a rule from the first without hesitation, from the second with a little, and from the third almost never. Whether a statement

The utility of teaching rules requires the occurrence of these circumstances. It is not useful to employ the shoulder rule if the student has a hand and arm of the wrong kind, no piano, no time to practice, and the like; and it would be equally futile to employ the rule for history in teaching the very young who have no interest in their own culture, no sense of the past, and no familiarity with clocks or calendars.

A third condition for the utility of employing a teaching rule is its harmony with other rules employed to further mastery in the same teaching situation. The employment of any given rule is more or less useful in light of the attitudes prevailing between teacher and student, the clarity of their communication, absence of incompatible instructions, the community's acceptance of the goal aimed at, and so on. These factors may be set forth either as circumstances in which teaching statements apply or as what teaching statements are about. Statements of the first kind, as we have seen, must be true if teaching rules are to be useful; but if these factors appear in teaching statements, then the rules they yield should be employed appropriately if any single rule is most usefully applied. The teaching statement, "Community respect sometimes accompanies mastery of piano technique" yields the rule, "To establish the technique, introduce the respect." And if this rule is applied, the shoulder rule will be more useful because it will be more likely to succeed.

There are general teaching statements which do not yield teaching rules directly. They do not mention the consequent of the teaching rule, that is, they do not mention what the rule peculiarly instructs the teacher to do in order to secure mastery. Rather, they state that certain general features accompany mastery of any kind. "Quick reward accompanies mastery," and "Motivation accom-

is a teaching statement or a statement of some circumstance which a teaching statement presupposes, is a matter of convenience, i.e. a matter of the ease with which one can introduce an item of the kind said to accompany mastery on some occasions. If the abnormality is not great, one might follow the rule "To achieve mastery, introduce a normal hand and arm by surgery." (Remember Robert Schumann.)

panies mastery" are examples. Rules can be derived from these general teaching statements by filling in more concrete values which fit the descriptions they contain, and then by changing the position of the components and altering the mood. They are of great importance to the teacher since they help to determine an entire cluster of rules all of which cooperate toward a single goal.

In order to discover the utility of employing a teaching rule, it is necessary, first, to discover the truth of its teaching statement; second, to discover the circumstances in which that statement is true; and third, to discover other rules toward the same goal frequently derived from general teaching statements whose employment enhances the utility of the rule under consideration. The first part of education, in the second sense of the word, the study of the excellence of teaching disciplines, is the effort to discover these conditions.

Employing even the most useful rules cannot assure a teacher's success. He must employ them where they apply; and in order to do this, he must know where they are applicable. He must not merely employ the shoulder rule, for example; he must also see that this particular student, in this particular situation, may benefit from its application. In order to do this, he must see that the circumstances which are presupposed by the truth of the rule's teaching statement hold for this particular student. Also, he must see that the employment of other rules enhances that of the shoulder rule; and for this, it is frequently necessary that he see that certain concrete things and actions correctly fit the general descriptions involved in general teaching statements. Something like this is true for teaching of all sorts. The conditions under which a teacher sees these things constitute many of the conditions of his effectiveness. The effort to discover them is the second part of education in the second sense.

But this study contains a third part. The excellence of a teaching discipline is not measured by its success alone, but by its success in doing something which is worth the moral while. People may be taught to master many subjects; and the excellence of each teaching discipline must be determined in the light not merely of the degree to which it secures its own objective, but in that of the moral value of a single life in which many goals of various teaching disciplines are realized. One person may be the focus of many different disciplines—of the teaching of swimming, of painting, of morals, of history, and so on; and the excellence of any one of these disciplines depends upon the virtue of his life which, in this way, incorporates the goals of all. The virtue of an individual life must be estimated, also, by reference to demands of larger groups to which it belongs. The excellence of teaching disciplines rests, in this way, upon the nature of the good life for individuals and for their societies; and the study of education is the investigation of the conditions for the moral value of teaching activities as well as for their success.

Education, in this sense of the word, is like a discipline in one respect; for it has a single goal, the discovery of the conditions for excellence in teaching activities. But its similarity extends no further. No unified body of rules governs the pursuit of its goal; on the contrary, it takes the form of a great number of very different procedures. The conditions for the utility of the shoulder rule, for example, may be sought in many different ways. To find out whether the feeling accompanies mastery, one may consult one's own experience, read autobiographies of performers, interview students, and carry out controlled experiments. These procedures are different, but each is relevant. And the ways in which the truth of any teaching statement is discovered surely are at least as numerous. Many different procedures, again, aid in the discovery of the circumstances which the truth of a teaching statement presupposes. The kind of body to which the shoulder statement applies is discovered by methods of observation and comparison. The culture's evaluation of piano performance may be revealed by interview, questionnaire, and sampling techniques; or by an historical investigation into the origin of its attitudes and institutions. Again the effect of employing one rule upon employing another may be determined by different methods. Whether a motivation rule makes the shoulder rule more useful, may be investigated by introspection, by biographical study, by simple observation, by controlled experiment, and so on. It is equally clear that different procedures are appropriate for ascertaining the conditions under which a teacher sees how to apply his rules for the ability to employ them in concrete situations.

The rules by which we ferret out the conditions for success in teaching activities, however various, are more like each other than those we follow to ascertain the conditions for their moral value. The first, at least, are all ways of investigating facts; and the conclusions we harvest with their use are subject to a single criterion, that of truth or probability. But the procedures for establishing the conditions under which a person or society possesses moral value are not exhausted by investigation of the facts concerning them; and the conclusions which they yield, statements of the good life and the manner in which teaching activities enter into it, are not subject to the criterion which governs the acceptability of statements of fact. The study of the conditions for the excellence of teaching activities, education in the second sense, is not a discipline; for while its goal is single, the paths to it, and the rules for following each, are very numerous indeed.

We have considered education as teaching activities and as the study of the conditions for their excellence. But there is a third use of the word in which we refer to a theory that describes teaching activities and that results from the study of the conditions for their excellence. In this third sense, "education" is a name for the theory of teaching activities. It is the theory of education in the first sense.

Theory of education contains statements of three kinds. First, it contains statements of the conditions for the utility of teaching rules. Among them we find teaching statements which are arrived at by methods of the sorts we have suggested; the evidence for them may be secured by the procedures of physiology, psychology, sociology, history, and what not. We find, also, statements of the circumstances in which teaching statements apply. For these, again, the methods of various sciences bring evidence—those of optics and neurology for understanding the lighting of the schoolroom, of history and economics for the social circumstances of the school or other teaching institutions, of psychology, sociology, and cultural anthropology for prevailing attitudes, and so on. Moreover, we find statements about the way in which the employment of one teaching rule affects the utility of employing another, and general statements telling us what sorts of things accompany mastery. Again, we find statements setting forth the conditions for the teacher's ability to apply his rules in a useful way. It is clear that all the statements in this first group must find their evidence through methods characterizing the various natural and social sciences.

The second group of statements in theory of education is made up of teaching rules; and the third includes statements of the good life for individuals and for societies which the employment of teaching rules advances. But there are a great many teaching rules. Which of them does the second group include? It is clear that the answer to this question is determined by that life for individuals and for societies which we fix upon as good. But concluding in favor of one among other candidates for moral allegiance depends upon a procedure which is not scientific. It depends upon a method, irrelevant to scientists, discussed by philosophers, and pursued by seers, prophets, and all of us on those occasions, all too rare, when we are making genuine moral decisions. In the third group we find statements based upon this method of moral reflection, and these statements admit into theory of education only those teaching rules whose employment makes an activity excellent, not merely successful. This limitation upon teaching rules, in turn, limits admission to the first group of statements also. There is an enormous number of teaching rules whose utility might be investigated, and statements of the conditions for whose utility might be a theme for theory of education. Rules for establishing mastery in murder, in building with gold, and in playing jokes on ocelots no doubt exist. But statements of the conditions for their utility do not occur in theory of education because the teaching activities which these rules govern are not admitted into the good life. Philosophical procedures determine what statements occur in the third group; and in this way, also, what teaching rules and what statements concerning their utility are found in the second and first, respectively. Theory of education rests upon the employment of philosophical methods determining the excellence of teaching disciplines, and upon scientific methods for determining the conditions under which these activities may succeed.

Is theory of education a discipline? Our answer must be in the negative if we mean by discipline an activity directed toward a goal and conducted in accord with a single set of rules. A theory is not an activity at all. But there is another use of the word according to which it is applied to any field of knowledge or organized body of statements. In this sense, theory of education is a discipline. For the statement of the good life orders all the others by showing what teaching rules the theory may contain, and consequently, what statements for utility of rules it may admit. The order may extend into detail. It may be that in the light of moral principles, some teaching rules are subordinated to others as are the masteries they foster; and that some statements of the conditions for their successful employment, consequently, are subordinated to other such statements. Theory of education is a discipline; its parts are organized by moral principles.

Conceived as teaching activities, education is many disciplines. Each teaching activity follows a set of rules for achieving a goal. If it succeeds, it expresses the ability to see how the rules apply. Regarded as the study of the excellence of teaching activities, education is not a discipline, for many different rules must be pursued in order to achieve its goal—a discovery of the conditions for excellence of teaching activities. Thought of as a theory, education is not a discipline in the first sense of that word, because it is not an activity at all. But theory of education is a discipline in a second sense, for it is an organized body of statements—a system formed by selecting teaching rules and statements of the conditions for their utility according as they make for the realization of the good life for persons and societies.

I have spoken as if the study of teaching activities were, itself, a highly organized activity, as if all those who are in any way concerned in the study were intent upon contributing to a clearer understanding of the conditions for its excellence. I have spoken, also, as if theory of education were a *fait accompli,* as if we possessed a body of rules and teaching statements whose articulation were clearly illuminated by the bright light of a moral insight. Both these ways of speaking may be misleading. Probably, we are not investigating many of the conditions for excellence in teaching; certainly, our efforts are somewhat scattered and isolated from each other. Probably, we do not know many of the statements which theory of education would include; certainly, no one can be quite sure, in view of our scattered efforts, what parts of it we can legitimately assert. But if the study of teaching disciplines is not itself a discipline, it may yield a theory which is one. "The prospect of a theory of education," Kant said, "is a glorious ideal, and it matters little if we are unable to realize it immediately." And if I have spoken in the indicative, I have thought all along in the optative mood.

But why, in any case, do we ask whether education is a discipline? Do we regard teaching activities, their study, and the theory it may yield as important? Do we want to say they are disciplines because the word drives their importance home, making people anxious to support them? Or do we regard them as trivial or unworthy? Do we want to say they are not disciplines because the negative phrase makes their triviality or unworthiness evident, directing people to disregard or curtail them? In either case we should remember that the language we employ for describing education can do no more than set it forth, and that while the words we use may reflect the value we place on education, they make what they describe neither more nor less important than it is. The value of education is a matter of the role it plays in our lives; and while this role is what a true description makes evident, it is an altogether different thing from the words we use to make it so. Employing the word "discipline" in a positive or negative description of education does not, as such, justify any treatment of that subject.

I have held that education as teaching activities is the subject matter for education as a study, and that education as a study may yield education as a theory. By exhibiting typical uses of "discipline," I have argued that education in the first sense should be described as many disciplines and that in the second sense, although it has a subject matter and a goal, it should not be described as a discipline. I have suggested that in the third sense, education should be described as a discipline, but one of a generically different sort. But the importance or unimportance of teaching activities, of their study, and of their theory is a matter to be argued, if at all, in another place.

COMMENTS   *Frederick A. Siegler*

Dr. Price claims that there are three features essential to all teaching activities. First, every teaching activity involves a goal. Second, the teacher must have "rules for achieving mastery of his subject." Third, the teacher must attempt "to employ the rules as guides to the achievement of mastery." He concludes that "teaching consists in an activity which expresses the intention to use rules as guides to the mastery of some subject."

These features are *sometimes* found in teaching. Let us say that Jones wants his son to learn to play chess; he has formulated some rules for teaching; and he intends to employ the rules.

But this case is quite different from a variety of others in which teaching takes place. Consider a situation in which a woman orders her husband not to drink at home on the grounds that he is teaching the children the wrong sort of thing to do. A woman might say that it was her husband who taught the children all their bad habits, such as putting their elbows on the table or talking with their mouths full. She might say that he taught them good things, too, such as reading the newspaper every day and the Bible every night. He might have taught the children these things merely by doing them; and they learned, for better or for worse, by watching and being with him. The husband need not have had any teaching goals in mind. He might not have been aware that he had taught them such things. He might not have meant to teach such things. He might be sorry that he taught them. He taught them, however, not with teaching goals or teaching rules in mind, but unwittingly.

An overemphasis of certain kinds of highly formalized teaching activities leads to a misleading analysis of the wide variety of teaching activities, and it might lead to overlooking many important varieties of teaching. People learn jokes, apt expressions, and manners from people who have not the least interest in teaching, methods or rules for producing mastery, or intentions to employ rules for the production of masteries.

Another form of teaching is teaching oneself. A man who is teaching himself to ride a bicycle or to paint in oils may have a goal in mind, but he need not have a clear set of rules for producing competence in riding or oil painting. Never having done these things before, he might learn by experimenting—by trial and error. And if the concept of having rules has any boundary lines, it must rule out having no rules, such as doing things by trial and error.

But now let us return to the case of Jones teaching his son to play chess. Assume that Dr. Price's three features are present. Jones has a goal—to teach his son to play chess; he has formulated some rules for achieving the goal; and, finally, he intends to employ these rules as guides to the mastery of the subject. I have already suggested that these three features are not necessary for every teaching activity. I have gone so far (perhaps too far) as to suggest that none of them are necessary. But now I wonder whether they are sufficient for calling something "teaching." I do not think so. Certainly Jones might have the goal, the rules, and the intention to employ the rules, but never actually do any teaching at all. Also he could write the rules on a paper headed with the words, "Rules which I intend to employ in teaching my son to play chess." Surely this activity—writing the rules under this heading—would normally "express the intention to use rules as guides for the mastery of some subject." But "anyone who engages in activity of this kind" is not *eo ipso* teaching.

Furthermore, not just *any* rules will suffice. Say Jones writes down the following rules: "Eat lettuce roots, carrots, and drink plenty of beer." Suppose that Jones *believes* that these are rules for teaching his son to play chess. Even if Jones does have a goal and *these* rules, and actually employs them on his son, we should not call the activity one of teaching. At best we should say that Jones *thinks* that he is teaching, but is terribly misguided. It is not that he is teaching chess improperly, but that he is not teaching chess at all.

Dr. Price says, "If we did not know it to be true that the shoulder feeling sometimes accompanies proficiency, employing the teaching rule it yields would be as useless as employing any that we might merely imagine; and teaching piano technique could not be distinguished from pretending to teach it." (Pretending to teach may involve employing rules which one knows to be ineffective, but from this it does not follow that a teacher must know that a given rule is effective in order for it to be effective.) What is important is that the rule truly is effective. Success in employing a rule depends on the efficacy of the rule, but not on the teacher's or anybody else's knowledge of the efficacy.

Dr. Price might prefer to say that if the rules are not effective then the teaching cannot be successful, but also that if the rules are grossly inappropriate for the subject matter, there is no teaching at all. His view would then be that successful teaching requires knowing certain rules which are adequate for the subject matter, and knowing how to apply these rules. The more adequate the rules and the more the teacher knows how to apply the rules, the more successful the teaching will be.

I would like to examine the phrase, "having rules for the mastery of a subject matter."

Consider a man who teaches competence in chess. Is the phrase attempting to suggest that he *must* have a set of rules which he employs in order to teach? He might have formulated a set of rules, but this does not seem necessary. Say the teacher merely sits down and plays with his pupils. They know the rudiments before he takes them. They learn by the experience of playing with him. In this case the teacher would not have a ready answer to the question, "What rules do you employ in teaching competence in chess?" He might reply, "I have no rules; I just play." This same answer might be given by a person who is by himself perfecting his skill at chess, golf, or piano. A chess teacher might sometimes simply play with his pupil, sometimes point out flaws in the pupil's strategy, sometimes point out his own strategy, sometimes both, and so on. But when asked, "What rules do you employ in teaching?" he might have no ready answer. In these cases I think that it is misleading to say the teacher *has rules* which he employs.

On the other hand, an observer (education expert) may *see* a pattern, regularity, or method *in* the activities of a teacher. Yet, again the teacher may have no ready answer to the question, "What rules do you employ in teaching?" My teaching, for example, might display some pattern, regularity, or method; yet I should have no ready answer to the question, "What rules?" I should be surprised to find a report entitled "Siegler's Rules for Teaching Philosophy." I should probably be surprised (perhaps enlightened) at the contents. The observer could not conclude that in my teaching I am trying to employ rules for the mastery of philosophy. The expert may conclude that my teaching reveals a pattern, but it would be inaccurate to say that I planned or intended such a pattern. My teaching might *accord* with a method, but it need not be for the *sake* of that method.

Teaching, then, does not require knowing how to recite rules for teaching. Nor does it require knowing how to recite the proper rules for teaching. Dr. Price does say that the "rules sometimes lurk in the background, known in the way we all know the rules of our mother tongue, without thought or care." But first, it does not seem right to say that knowing how to speak one's mother tongue involves knowing rules. One learns to talk long before one learns rules of grammar, and rules of grammar are not rules of language. But secondly, Dr. Price seems to have a notion of quite explicit rules, for he often speaks of examining the "utility of the rules" which teachers employ; and more important, he speaks of the "ability to see how to apply [rules]."

There is something wrong with the claim that knowing how to teach, or knowing how to speak a language, requires having certain rules, plus knowing how to apply these rules. For if knowing how to teach requires having rules, plus knowing how to apply them, then knowing how to apply them would seem to require having further rules, plus knowing how to apply them. That is to say, if knowing how to teach spelling requires having rules for teaching, plus knowing how to apply the rules for teaching, then does it not follow (by the same token) that knowing how to apply the rules for teaching requires having further rules for applying rules for teaching, plus knowing how to apply these new rules? But if all knowing how requires rules, then knowing how to apply rules requires further rules. But if this were so, we should never get any teaching done at all. And that would be a paradoxical conclusion.

Of course, that cannot be exactly what Dr. Price has in mind. He might suggest that the teacher just knows how to apply the teaching rules and that he does not have to have *rules* for knowing how to apply the teaching rules. But if this is so, then why could a person not just know how to teach spelling without having to have any *rules* for knowing how to teach spelling? And then what would be the point of talk about rules at all?

Though the practice of teaching need not involve the intentional employment of rules for mastery of a subject, it is certainly the province of the study of education to study the practice of teaching in order to discover patterns or methods of successful teaching. Education experts who investigate the activities of excellent teachers may well find techniques and methods in these activities. They may find certain methods of teaching which are always successful. But they may find no such things.

Techniques developed by experts of education may be derived from the examination of successful teaching operations and may involve an amount of speculation on education, too. The application of such techniques is probably most important in the area of elementary school teaching, where the subject matter to be taught is relatively simple and restricted and well understood by the teacher. For an elementary school teacher there is no problem of finding time to do research in spelling and arithmetic, but there is often a problem of how to teach certain skills so that the student can go on with these skills to higher education. The study of techniques and of the overall education structure could be of particular help here. Teaching skills is important, but how the skills are taught is also important. While a child can learn to count on his fingers and toes, he can also learn to count by employing concepts which will not only enable him to work out a professor's income tax, but will enable him to go on into higher mathematics.

One hopes, of course, that the interest in, discovery of, and promulgation of teaching methods does not obscure the importance of enthusiasm for teaching and mastery of the subject matter, and does not discourage or inhibit naturally gifted teachers. Procrustes could manage neither a hotel nor a school board for very long.

What relevance have teaching methods in the universities? Should a teacher of history of philosophy be required to employ the latest methods of teaching in his field? Here I can make only a few general comments. In advanced education there is (and probably ought to be more) greater emphasis on doing rather than teaching. Or perhaps this should be put: Teaching is by doing. The teacher sets standards of care and precision; the student endeavors to meet the standards of academic work. The gap between the teacher and the student is narrow and probably ought to be narrower. Here, it is important that the teacher be good at what he does, be he historian, philosopher, or physicist. Education is more and more up to the student himself. He can watch and work with competent academic men, and learn from them and with them, and decide how much more of it he wants or can take. Here, talk about teaching rules and knowing how to apply teaching rules seems less interesting.

One final point. Dr. Price suggests that, although the methods for discovering rules for teaching are empirical and scientific, the methods for discovering the right things to teach are neither empirical nor scientific. This is, of course, an old and a new story. But I am inclined to believe that, if we were clear about what is meant by empirical and scientific, we would find that the distinction between the empirical and scientific and between non-empirical and non-scientific is less clear than the more homely distinction between simple and difficult problems. The problems of methods *and* the problems of value in education both fall into the latter category. And, as with most difficult problems, the solutions require a good deal of thought, talk, and experiment. Consequently, it is probably a very good thing that these problems are discussed by both theorists of education and ordinary practitioners.

III

Is Education a Discipline?

ISRAEL SCHEFFLER

I. INTRODUCTION

Does the *enterprise* of education rest upon a *discipline* of education? Is there some autonomous branch of knowledge underlying educational practice? Does the art of education derive its guiding principles from a distinctive realm of theory?

These questions are most serious when they refer, not to the current state of the sciences, but to the principle of the matter. Granted that we do not now have a discipline of education, is there not necessarily such a discipline to be developed or discovered by investigation? Does not the hope of real educational progress depend, moreover, upon the success with which such investigation is carried forward? This rhetorical way of putting the matter is disarmingly simple and has undeniable persuasiveness. Yet we will do well to examine the grounds on which an affirmative answer might be defended.

II. EDUCATIONAL PRACTICE

The practice of education is surely a discipline, it might be said. Some ways of educating are preferable to others; there must be rules distinguishing the better from the worse practices and enjoining us to choose the better. Educational skill is, furthermore, not instinctive but rather the product of training and experience, leading to a mastery of these rules. Such training and experience, as well as the finished art of the master teacher, serve, finally, to discipline the educator as all art disciplines the artist, through the continual challenge to exercise discretion and judgment, patience and foresight, to sacrifice himself in the quest for excellence, to perfect his understanding and love of his material.[1]

This account of the practice of education is certainly plausible. Yet it does not have the slightest tendency to establish the fact that the practice rests upon some autonomous branch of knowledge distinctive to it. That rules govern educational practice may be sufficient ground for declaring such practice to be a discipline, in one sense of this word. It is no ground for supposing these rules to be drawn from a unique theoretical discipline, in another sense of this word. Engineering is governed by rules, but these rules are not drawn from a special science of engineering.

That educational skill is a result of training and experience may provide another reason for holding the practice of education to be a discipline. It gives no support, however, to the supposition that there must be a distinctive branch of science underlying the practice. Medical skill is a product of training and experience, though it draws upon a host of intellectual disciplines. That medicine is a practical discipline does not imply the existence of a unique science of medicine.

There is, finally, an important analogy between serious teaching and serious art. Each disciplines the agent through challenge. It is, however, fallacious to infer from the fact that an activity possesses disciplinary value, that it must therefore rest upon a distinctive discipline of inquiry. There is no science of poetry, though poetry disciplines and civilizes. Nor does painting, for all its creative challenge, presuppose an autonomous science of painting. We must, in short, be careful to distinguish the ways in which we

1. See, in this connection, M. Black, "Education as Art and Discipline," *Ethics*, LIV (1944), 290–94; reprinted in I. Scheffler, ed., *Philosophy and Education* (Boston: Allyn & Bacon, 1958).

apply the word discipline to activities in general, from the ways in which we apply it to branches of knowledge in particular, and we must avoid fallacious inferences from the one sort of case to the other.

III. THE EDUCATIONAL REALM

Let us then resolve to speak here of theoretical disciplines exclusively—of branches of knowledge or bodies of science. Each such discipline, it may be said, strives to offer a complete, systematic account of some realm of things in the world. It seeks a comprehensive body of true principles describing and explaining the realm it takes as its proper object. The realm of physical things is the object of the discipline of physics, whose province thus embraces all significant truths concerning physical objects.

Consider now the realm of things involved in educational processes: schools, subjects, ideas, social practices and traditions, students, teachers, methods, and curricula. Surely this important realm must form the proper object of some single theoretical discipline, comprehending all significant general truths about the processes of education. Unless we are to abandon the assumption that the world is ordered, we must suppose that there is, for each realm, and, in particular, for the educational realm, some special and exclusive discipline, comprising within its scope all those principles capable of describing and explaining the peculiar orders which it exemplifies.

This argument takes the view that there is a one-to-one correlation between realms and disciplines, that not only does each discipline apply to a unique realm, but that each realm supports at least one, and at most one, discipline. If it were not so wrong, this view would be most appealing in its symmetry, embodying, as it does, the time-honored notion that reality and discourse are mirror images of one another.[2]

2. For a general discussion, see N. Goodman, "The Way the World Is," *Review of Metaphysics,* XIV (1960), 48–56.

Unfortunately, however, a variety of disciplines may be supported by elements of the same realm, while some realms seem patently to support no discipline at all. It is not the case that if we were to collect all the significant general truths concerning elements of any given realm, they would fill one and only one box, representing *the* discipline of that realm. Indeed, this notion would appear to harbor a contradiction. For if there were a box for realm A and another for realm B, there would need to be still a third for the realm consisting of A + B, containing truths belonging, on the theory before us, exclusively to the first two boxes.

Much of the appeal of the theory derives from the example of physics, whose domain allegedly comprises *all* truths descriptive and explanatory of the realm of physical objects. But the appeal of this example evaporates once we take a good look at the contents of the physical realm. Some physical objects are, after all, linguistic tokens, some are fossils, some are plants or animals, some are people. Even the hardiest physicalist will find it embarrassing to maintain that the truths comprising linguistics, paleontology, biology, anthropology, and psychology belong, even in principle, to the single discipline of physics. And while chemistry is perhaps in principle easier to think of as reducible to physics, it is not (as construed now and in prior years) *actually* thus reducible though it applies to the same realm. It becomes obvious upon reflection that disciplines quite distinct in content and manner of expression may be supported by the same realm of things.[3] At its best, physicalism is thus a doctrine concerning the elements to which disciplines apply, rather than a doctrine claiming exhaustiveness for the discipline of physics.

If the realm of physical objects is taken as our model for the educational realm, we have no reason to suppose that there is at

3. The independence of ontology from the conceptual apparatus of a theory is discussed in W. V. Quine, *From a Logical Point of View* (Cambridge, Mass.: Harvard University Press, 1953), particularly Chapter VII. A criticism of the notion that we explain *objects* is contained in the last section of my "Explanation, Prediction, and Abstraction," *British Journal for the Philosophy of Science,* VII (1957), 293–309.

most one theoretical discipline of education, comprising all those general descriptive and explanatory truths concerning the elements of education. Nor, considering certain other realms as examples, do we have any reason to suppose that every realm must support at least one discipline, on pain of violating some general assumption of an ordered universe. There is no discipline associated with the realm of chairs, but this does not mean that the mechanical behavior of chairs presents a baffling mystery to our sense of order. Chairs, as well as all other classes of physical objects, fall under the general principles of physics. It is clearly fallacious to infer, from the fact that every discipline takes some realm of things as its object, that therefore every realm of things must be the object of some discipline. If there is, in fact, no special discipline of education, it does not in the least follow that the realm of education must remain opaque to our understanding.

IV. EDUCATIONAL PHENOMENA

We have criticized the notion of a one-to-one correlation between theoretical disciplines and realms of things. Disciplines may differ, we have said, despite the fact that they are associated with the same range of objects. Perhaps the reason is that they give accounts of different classes of phenomena manifested by these self-same objects or, alternatively, of different classes of aspects or properties possessed by them.

The idea is a natural one. Consider John Smith. His weight is a physical datum, his pulse a biological datum, and his conversation a psychological datum. He is simultaneously subject to physical, biological, and psychological analysis. What is more plausible than to suppose that, in addition to the concrete John Smith before us, there are a variety of related Platonic entities to be reckoned with, namely, the physical, the biological, and the psychological phenomena manifested by him? Each such set of phenomena, it might be said, forms the basis of some discipline applicable to

Smith, providing an ethereal bridge between Smith the object and the truths by which he is described within this particular discipline.

The variety of disciplines, on this view, thus arises out of the variety of types of phenomena. To each such type corresponds a single discipline, and every discipline corresponds to some single type. The existence of educational phenomena thus guarantees, at least in principle, a unique discipline of education, though, admittedly, any range of objects manifesting educational phenomena will certainly be manifesting other sorts of phenomena as well, and so be analyzable by several disciplines at once.

There is a certain attractiveness to this view, and it accords well with much of our ordinary thinking and talking; but it will not withstand serious analysis. Objections analogous to those previously discussed present themselves immediately. Not every set of aspects, properties, or phenomena supports a separate discipline. If there is no science of the class of chairs, neither is there a science of the phenomenon of chairhood. Nor is it the case that at most one discipline formulates the truth concerning any given set of phenomena. It is, to be sure, undeniable that linguistic studies, for example, do not address themselves to the physical properties of their subject matter, but such properties surely enter into disciplines other than physics, for example, chemistry and biology.

Formally, too, the contradiction noted above lurks here as well. If the class of phenomena K and the class of phenomena L have unique disciplines associated with them, and there is also a unique discipline for the class $K + L$, either some truths fall into two boxes or some box is not completely filled. At this point, however, the possibility of a new philosophical move presents itself. We may declare that we have an independent criterion for determining "pure" classes of phenomena and that this criterion prevents the formation of $K + L$, upon which the troublesome contradiction depends. Putting the matter another way, the one-to-one correlation of disciplines and phenomenal classes is now proposed to hold only for pure phenomenal classes, as determined by our supposed independent criterion. This criterion rules out, for example, the class of physical-biological phenomena, recognizing only the two classes of purely physical and purely biological phenomena. This move was inappropriate before, with respect to objects, for the notion of a purely biological or purely physical object is inconceivable. The notion of a purely biological or physical aspect, property, or phenomenon, however, is not at all inconceivable.

The Platonizing of our problem thus does accomplish something new by comparison with the previous formulation. In particular, it avoids the inconsistency noted, and it allows several disciplines to apply to the same realm of objects, claiming only a one-to-one correlation with pure classes of phenomena associated with this realm. But it fails to remove the other objections noted. For it will still be difficult to maintain that every pure class of phenomena supports a discipline. And it will still be true that more than one discipline is related to a given pure class of phenomena as, for example, anthropology and sociology are both concerned with social phenomena. Further, it is no longer clear that we still have an argument for the existence of an educational discipline, since it is not clear that educational phenomena are pure.

It might be said that at least one of the above criticisms is unfair: social phenomena are not pure; they must be split into anthropological and sociological phenomena, each group supporting at most one discipline. But how do we know this? What, after all, *is* our criterion for determining pure classes of phenomena? What, indeed, is a phenomenon, aspect, or property, as distinct from the thing which manifests it and the word which attributes it? [4] Presumably, the mass of a particular painting by Monet is one of its physical phenomena or aspects, while its being an instance of French impressionism is not. Presumably, Khrushchev's power is a sociological property, unlike his height, vol-

4. See, in this connection, N. Goodman, "On Likeness of Meaning," *Analysis,* X (1949), 1–7, reprinted in *Semantics and the Philosophy of Language,* ed., L. Linsky (Urbana: University of Illinois Press, 1952), and M. White, *Toward Reunion in Philosophy* (Cambridge, Mass.: Harvard University Press, 1956).

ume, and chemical composition, which are not. Are not these decisions, however, perfectly parallel to the judgments by which we decide that the term "mass" is a physical term while the term "instance of French Impressionism" is not, that the term "power" belongs to the vocabulary of sociology, whereas the terms employed in formulating height, volume, and chemical descriptions do not? This question gives rise to the nagging suspicion that the language of phenomena is a parasite on the language of language, that phenomena have no independent life but are projected on the world by the terms we use, that they are mere shadows cast on objects by our descriptions of them. Why not clarify the situation by eliminating this shadow world completely, and focussing our attention directly on the language in which our accepted descriptions and explanations of things are expressed?

V. EDUCATIONAL TERMS

We began by trying to construe theoretical disciplines in terms of peculiar realms of objects and found this course unsatisfactory. The alternative attempt to attach such disciplines to distinctive classes of pure phenomena turned out to be equally frustrating, for new as well as old reasons. Shall we fare better by turning from objects and phenomena to words?

Some clear pitfalls in this new course are immediately evident. We must not, for example, proceed to explain the disciplines as characterized by special vocabularies, and then blithely go on to delimit these vocabularies in terms of what is required to account for distinct realms of phenomena or objects. For this would raise the old difficulties again. Nor must we characterize the discipline of physics, for instance, as one formulated in physical terms—understanding by physical term a term which is used in formulating physics. For such a procedure would be clearly circular. What then *can* be done?

The attractiveness of the present idea lies in the fact that the several theoretical disciplines may be construed as several bodies of systematized information, each such body presumably expressed by a distinctive linguistic apparatus. Assume, for simplicity's sake, a common core of logical terms and a common syntax for all disciplines. The extralogical vocabulary of each will then differ from that of each other in at least some degree. Thus, for example, biology, but not physics, will contain the extralogical term "cell," though both share a common logical structure. Some degree of overlap in vocabularies is thus compatible with the distinctiveness of each, taken as a whole. Can we not then specify the domain of each discipline as what is expressible by means of the extralogical vocabulary associated with it, with the help of logic and in accord with the assumed standard syntax? And is not a discipline of education thus guaranteed by the fact that the vocabulary of education is, at least in part, distinctive?

There are complex refinements to be made before the present idea can be put with even minimal clarity. Consider, for example, the extralogical vocabulary of biology; let us designate this vocabulary as B. Now let us designate the extralogical vocabulary of chemistry as C. We may reasonably assume that B overlaps C, that is, that certain extralogical terms belong to both the biological and the chemical vocabularies. How shall we now classify a statement S, whose extralogical constituents are all drawn from the area of overlap? Shall we, in particular, assign S to the discipline of biology or to the discipline of chemistry?

We may attempt to settle this question by introducing some notion of presuppositional order among the disciplines. We assume, for example, that physics presupposes logic, that chemistry presupposes physics and is in turn presupposed by biology. Now if S is composed of extralogical terms wholly drawn from the overlap of the biological and chemical vocabularies, but not at all from the overlap of both of these with physics, then we assign S to chemistry, since biology presupposes chemistry. In Morton White's phrase, S contains no *specifically* biological terms, but only specifically chemical terms, except for logic.[5]

What shall we now do with a statement of another sort, T, which *does* contain some specifically biological terms, as well as some specifically chemical terms, but no other extralogical terms? Here we may follow the rule recently suggested by White, that a statement is to be classified under a given discipline if, besides containing terms specific to that discipline, all other contained terms are specific to disciplines presupposed by it.[6] Thus T is to be assigned to biology.

Let us here waive the difficult question as to how the order of presupposition is to be interpreted, as well as all other problems arising out of the foregoing refinements. The basic idea is now that the province of a discipline is to be construed in terms of its specific extralogical vocabulary as well as its standing in the order of presupposition. Does it not now follow, from the existence of a specific educational vocabulary, that there must be a discipline of education?

Before we say yes to the last question, we must look critically at the basic idea underlying it. As a matter of fact, the general proposal has untenable consequences. Suppose, for example, that the terms "table" and "round" are each definable in physical terminology. Then the true statement, "Some tables are not round," is expressible in the specific language of physics. Yet this statement surely does not belong to the discipline of physics. Indeed, if this statement were considered to belong to physics because translatable into physical terms, its negation, "All tables are round," would also belong to physics by the same token, and the discipline of physics would turn out self-contradictory. Neither statement, in fact, belongs to the body of physical theories and laws, nor does either

5. See M. White, "Historical Explanation," *Mind,* LII (1943), reprinted with Postscript, in P. Gardiner, *Theories of History* (Chicago: Free Press, 1959), where the attempt is made to determine the status of history as an independent discipline.

6. See his reply to a query by the present writer, in P. Gardiner, *Theories of History,* p. 372.

one follow from these. The term "table," though definable in physical terms, is, moreover, not a term that can properly be said to belong to the discipline of physics. It does not now figure in the formulation of physical laws or theories, nor is it ever likely to do so. The range of a discipline, if these reflections are correct, is considerably narrower than what is theoretically expressible by means of the discipline's distinctive linguistic apparatus. Much of what is thus expressible falls outside the discipline, and two disciplines may conceivably share the same apparatus. The range of a discipline thus seems to be a function, not of the expressive power of a given linguistic apparatus, but rather of the availability of a body of laws and theories which have been formulated and established within its scope. The point may be put in terms of the reduction of one discipline to another. If one discipline is to be reduced to a second, it will not in general be enough to show its terminology to be wholly definable by means of the second discipline's terminology. It will, in addition, be necessary to show its principles to be derivable from those of the second discipline.[7] This is another way of saying that the range of a discipline is set by a body of laws and theories, rather than by a particular vocabulary of terms.

While the derivation of a given statement from the principles of a particular discipline shows that the statement has indeed been reduced to, and hence belongs to, that discipline, it does *not* follow that every unreduced statement belongs to *some other* discipline. Recall our recent statement, "Some tables are not round." Though we may here assume each of its extralogical terms to be definable by means of the vocabulary of physics, it does not, I have argued, belong to the discipline of physics. Nor is there any necessity of supposing that, because it falls outside physics, it must therefore fall within the scope of some other discipline.

Note that, in the statement we have just considered, every

7. See E. Nagel, "The Meaning of Reduction in the Natural Sciences," in *Science and Civilization,* ed., R. C. Stauffer (Madison: University of Wisconsin Press, 1949), and *The Structure of Science* (New York and Burlingame: Harcourt, Brace, and World, 1961).

extralogical term is definable in physical terminology and yet the statement as a whole is not "significant" in any theoretical sense; it is not likely to figure as a principle of any scientific discipline, though it is true. In general, the fact that a term is definable within the language of a discipline in no way guarantees that there must be significant principles formulable with its help. Carl Hempel some years ago illustrated an argument of his by inventing the term "hage." [8] A person's "hage" is his height, in inches, multiplied by his age, in years. Now my hage happens to be 2,698. Assume that I can be identified by my present spatio-temporal position, within the language of physics. It is obvious that, though the object with this position can then be said, within physical terminology, to have a hage of 2,698, this statement is not part of the discipline of physics. There is, furthermore, surely no necessity that the term "hage" will be fruitful in the formulation of any theoretical or lawlike principle within any discipline, despite the fact that it is definable in physical terms by means of which significant principles are expressed. [9]

Is it not even more obvious that disciplines cannot be created simply by producing new terms not definable within the vocabularies of established disciplines? Assume that educational terminology is distinctive, and thus allows us to express more than could be expressed without it. The crucial question remains whether this surplus is scientifically significant: Are there laws and theories forming a systematic and comprehensive body of assertions that are both expressible by means of this terminology and true, or at least, interesting in the scientific sense, and well supported? This condition is not necessarily met by every term. The fact that a term belongs to none of the hitherto established disciplines does not therefore guarantee that there must be some as-yet-undiscov-

8. C. G. Hempel, *Fundamentals of Concept Formation in Empirical Science* (Chicago: University of Chicago Press, 1952), p. 46. I have here taken the liberty of specifying inches rather than Hempel's millimeters.

9. By "principles" I here intend lawlike principles rather than bare generalizations. See N. Goodman, *Fact, Fiction, and Forecast* (Cambridge, Mass.: Harvard University Press, 1955).

ered discipline to which it will belong. Whether the condition will in fact be met in a given case is determinable, if at all, by investigation rather than by a priori arguments. The mere distinctiveness of educational terminology, were it established, would not in itself guarantee the existence of a discipline of education.

VI. EDUCATIONAL PRINCIPLES

I have suggested that disciplines are dependent on the availability of established scientific principles, that is, theories and laws, and that the terms of a discipline are those by means of which such principles are formulated. Does this imply that there is no connection between a given discipline and terms or statements that fall outside it? I think the answer is No. For to suppose that there is no connection is to construe the disciplines as completely isolated and self-contained. It is to deny the applicability of the disciplines to the concrete affairs of everyday life.

To illustrate: I have above suggested that the term "table" does not belong to the discipline of physics in the sense that it does not represent a fruitful category in the formulation of physical principles. But imagine that someone drops a lighted cigar on my new coffee table and burns it. The question, Why did my new coffee table show a burn when I came back into the parlor with the cheese? is a question to which physics supplies a relevant answer. Suitably supplemented with the particulars of the case, physical principles explain the disaster, despite the fact that physics includes no laws of the burning of new coffee tables nor references to cheese or parlors. The term "abstract painting" is not, I suppose, even definable (at least in any obvious way) in physical terms, but physics will explain why a particular abstract painting fell from the wall yesterday. The terms peculiar to common affairs may belong to no discipline at all, but they normally figure in applying the disciplines to life. This they do in helping to formulate both the initial problems arising in practice, and those particulars which serve to bring problematic cases within the scope of disciplinary principles.

Suppose, now, that the terms peculiar to educational institutions and practices never yield a discipline of education in the sense outlined. Does this imply that education is cut off from all established disciplines, and must forever lack theoretical illumination? If the previous considerations are correct, the answer must clearly be in the negative. The problems of education, the questions arising in educational practice, will be framed in familiar educational terms. Whatever explanatory principles are at all relevant will receive their educational applications through being linked with these terms. The latter may not figure explicitly within the principles themselves, but to suppose these principles therefore irrelevant is to suppose an absurdity. It is to suppose, in effect, that these principles are generally useless because generally inapplicable.

A crucial issue, it thus seems to me, is whether we can establish reliable principles to explain how and why children learn, schools develop, curricula change, ideals conflict, perceptions alter, societies differ, standards of taste and culture are formed. That *any* discipline is likely to be developed capable of answering these questions systematically and reliably is still a matter of some controversy. Ernest Nagel, a distinguished student of logical and methodological issues in the social sciences, has recently written that

> In no area of social inquiry has a body of general laws been established, comparable with outstanding theories in the natural sciences in scope of explanatory power or in capacity to yield precise and reliable predictions. . . . Many social scientists are of the opinion, moreover, that the time is not yet ripe even for theories designed to explain systematically only quite limited ranges of social phenomena. . . . To a considerable extent, the problems investigated in many current centers of empirical social research are admittedly problems of moderate and often unimpressive dimensions. . . . In short, the social sciences today possess no wide ranging systems of explanations judged as adequate by a majority of professionally competent stu-

dents, and they are characterized by serious disagreements on methodological as well as substantive questions.[10]

The problem, it seems to me, is thus to advance the state of social inquiry—in particular, of all those studies which seem likely to yield explanatory principles relevant to the concerns of education.[11] Whether, however, it turns out that one or several theoretical disciplines develop, and whether any of these is a discipline of education specifically, seem to me quite unimportant issues.

As educators, we will continue to ask all sorts of questions arising in the course of our work. If the arguments presented above are at all convincing, we ought not to isolate ourselves from attempts to formulate principles relevant to our work, no matter what their disciplinary labels. Nor ought we to build our professional identity upon the faith that a unique discipline of education will one day be found. Rather, we should encourage relevant investigations by psychologists, anthropologists, sociologists, economists, educationists, and still others, and we should strive to link them with the concerns of schooling. There is surely enough substance in such an enterprise to support a genuine and important professional identity, indeed, several such identities. If it turns out that, in the place of a unique discipline of education, we get a variety of systematized laws and principles *applicable* to the practice of education, I cannot see that we will have serious cause for complaint.

COMMENTS *James E. McClellan*

The topic of this conference is very odd. Mr. Scheffler's paper has not eliminated the oddness. If properly read, his paper reveals the

10. E. Nagel, *The Structure of Science*, pp. 447–49.

11. See the related comments in my *The Language of Education* (Springfield: Charles C. Thomas Co., 1960), Chapter IV, pp. 71–75.

oddness so clearly that one may hope no future conference on this topic will have to be called. I return to an evaluation of Mr. Scheffler's paper at the end of my remarks. I want to talk first about discipline, second about disciplines and education, and then on to an evaluation of Mr. Scheffler's paper.

The term discipline has a variety of meanings. Mr. Scheffler has singled out the meaning most relevant to the topic we are considering, viz., the sense in which discipline is closely connected with scientific laws and theories. Why is this meaning most relevant? Not because it is the most usual or visible. Likely, the most usual meaning for the "discipline of X" is the administrative one. Universities have to be divided up somehow, and in America we tend to make the division by department, rather than by the teaching or residential college, the most significant one. In some other countries the college or faculty may be administratively a more significant unit than the department, and in those countries the question of what is or is not a discipline may not appear so important as it does to some Americans.

The assumption that each department follows one and only one discipline is quite absurd. Most universities have small but jealously independent departments of geography, but Harvard, so I am told, does not. One can say this situation proves that a discipline followed at most universities is ignored by America's oldest institution of higher learning, but it is more reasonable to conclude that Harvard merely found another way of cutting the cake more convenient. In this country, most students of symbolic logic, particularly if we restrict attention to multivalued and modal logics, are found in departments of philosophy. In the Soviet Union, students of these esoteric subjects are always found in departments of mathematics. The reason this time is not administrative convenience, but politics: considered as philosophy these studies are contemned as bourgeois formalism, but considered as part of mathematics they are entirely free from political judgment. The person who asks, "Yes, but to what disciplines do geography and symbolic logic really pertain?" has missed the point of my parables, and I shall not repeat them.

The most visible sense of discipline is the social one. A great many persons in this world are socially identified with one or more recognized branches of study. With the typically American genius for establishing voluntary associations for worthy purposes, we have organized learned societies by the score. If we want to *see* the discipline, we attend an annual meeting of the learned society, we read its journals, we watch the typical patterns of speech and action that distinguish its members from those of other learned societies. Sometimes when we speak of the "discipline of X"—as in the assertion, "We ought to have someone representing the discipline of X on this dissertation committee"—we are using discipline in its most visible sense. In some instances, for example, when X = history, the expression "department of X" will do just as well; in other instances, for example, when X = symbolic logic, it will not do just as well as "discipline of X." It is always ambiguous whether the expression "discipline of X" means the group of people who meet together, read each other's papers, hire each other's graduates, and do the other things members of disciplines do, or whether "discipline of X" means the particular knowledge or skill which is presumably requisite for membership in the group. I can not imagine this ambiguity causing any confusion.

Now Mr. Scheffler could have taken these other senses of discipline for the focus of his paper. Some interesting questions could arise. Is it just my own experience that leads me to believe that historians find it pleasant to say and hear "the discipline of history," whereas were a philosopher to say "the discipline of philosophy" very often he would be regarded as gauche or pretentious? And is not "the discipline of X" more likely to be said by non-Xists? "This topic seems to lie in the realm of the discipline of education," seems to suggest, though it does not imply, that the speaker is not an educationist.

In restricting his range to that sense in which discipline implies laws or theories, Mr. Scheffler has selected the most relevant sense. In rejecting the more usual or visible senses, he requires us for the nonce to forgo saying "the discipline of history," which seems to be a rather common, not to say vulgar, expression. There are many academic departments and learned societies to which we commonly extend the courtesy word discipline. Mr. Scheffler's restriction will require us to be more discriminating for the course of this discussion.

Mr. Scheffler, you see, is taking the position that we are not met here merely to engage in verbal by-play but to discuss an important problem. It is only when discipline implies some connection with scientific laws and theories that there is anything important to discuss. We already have departments, schools, and colleges of education. We have professional associations and learned societies of educationists. We have fairly clear notions of what one must know and know how to do if he is to be called a full-fledged educationist. In those senses, education *is* a discipline. Or, if you prefer, education is a family of related disciplines.

One more point about the word discipline. Mr. Scheffler asks that we "resolve to speak here of theoretical disciplines exclusively," and he mentions the discipline of physics presumably as the paradigm case of a theoretical discipline. I don't believe, however, that Mr. Scheffler would ever say *"the* theory of physics." A number of laws and theories are encompassed under the rubric "physics." These theories are more or less logically integrated: more at some times, less at others. At present experimental discoveries have outrun theoretical explanations in particle physics, whereas in astrophysics theoretically derived hypotheses await the appearance of techniques for experimental verification. The more basic theories in physics, of course, reappear in chemistry and in biology. To a degree, the line between disciplines is not precisely the line between theories; the former has an element of uneliminable historical arbitrariness, while the latter appears only after logical analysis shows how and where to draw it. This does not worry anyone, but it should remind us that even when we accept Mr. Scheffler's restrictions on discipline, the word is still not equivalent to the expression "scientific theory." Let me suggest the connection: the theoretical disciplines, as members of the class of all academic disciplines, are social, political, and administrative arrangements for accomplishing certain purposes. Like other disciplines, the theoretical disciplines have their center of gravity in the academic world and pursuit of knowledge as their primary purpose. As distinguished from other disciplines, the theoretical disciplines organize their findings more or less completely in scientific theories. By these criteria, law and medicine are not academic disciplines, for their centers of gravity lie outside the academic world, and the pursuit of knowledge is not their primary purpose. But theology, as opposed to the practice of religion, is an academic, some would say a theoretical, discipline. Physics is a theoretical discipline, sociology less so (this distinction *must* admit of degree), and history, the academic discipline par excellence, is scarcely theoretical at all. It is in this sense that we will use the word discipline henceforth.

If this tells us how we are to use "discipline," what shall we understand by the word "education"? It cannot be defined merely by pointing to certain features of the world, for we do not single out features except by description.[12] My first point: I can imagine no suitable description of education in which the question, Is education a discipline? can be answered in principle.

What does it mean to answer a question of the form, Is M an N? *in principle?* It means, I think, to show which of the three logical possibilities is the correct one. Given suitable definitions of M and N, then

1. Being an M logically requires being an N.
2. Being an M logically precludes being an N.
3. Being an M leaves it contingently possible to be or not be an N.

Is a cat an animal? is answered, in principle, by showing that

12. G. E. Anscombe (trans.), Ludwig Wittgenstein's *Phliosophical Investigations* (New York: Macmillan Co., 1953), 74 *et seq.*

it falls in logical case 1. Is the ellipse a rectilinear figure? is answered, in principle, by showing that it falls in logical case 2. Is the llama a swifter animal than the yak? is answered, in principle, by saying that this is the sort of question that would require, however unlikely the event, a race; that is, it falls in case 3.

Now these decisions are quite simple, for we have adequate and usual descriptions of the objects we call cats, animals, ellipses, and so on. Sometimes, for example with the question, Is God both benevolent and omniscient? it is more difficult to decide in which logical case to put the question. The answer depends on what we take to be the suitable description of God, omniscient being, and so forth.

But this question, Is education a discipline? resists any attempt to put it in one of these three categories. If we take discipline in Mr. Scheffler's sense, and if we take education to mean what he calls "the practice of education," then it follows for many reasons, including those outlined by Mr. Scheffler, that the question is not case 1. It also follows for the same reasons that the question is not case 2. Does this mean that it is case 3? I am not convinced that it does. The descriptions simply do not give any reason for holding that the question falls in any one of the three. Shall we then invent a case 4—it is indeterminate? Let us not. Let us simply say that of these three possibilities, until our definitions (or descriptions) are clearer, we simply do not know which one applies.

But why not get on with it—define education in sufficiently unambiguous terms, so that we can tell whether what we know or can find out about education does or does not organize itself into a scientific theory? Then we will know in which case to put this balky question!

How absurd. How can one tell in advance what terms will or will not organize themselves into scientific theories? The term "atom," we might guess from historical associations, is a natural for scientific theory. But Oedipus complex? Who would ever pick *that* for a key term in a scientific theory? Or take Mr. Scheffler's beautifully neutral, non-theoretical term "chair." I am now creating an extension of psychoanalytic theory: the term chair is to be used for the culturally approved object on which the buttocks are placed. The form of chair in any culture is a function of toilet-training practices and dependency relations. In Victorian culture, overstuffing the chair represents ———, while in contemporary America the Eames chair is a reflection of ———.

Is chair a theoretical term? This question is *in principle* unanswerable? If there is a theory in which the word chair appears (or appears essentially) then the question may be answered practically. But it is always possible to rewrite the theory so that chair disappears. And it is possible to rewrite existing theories so that chair appears: any three-dimensional lattice in probability theory shall be called a chair. But, you say, that is not the commonsense meaning of chair! Neither is *any* theoretical term exactly a commonsense concept. How far is too far?

To restate my first point: if a term we would unhesitatingly call an educational term appears in a set of statements we would unhesitatingly call a scientific theory—then we still have no answer in principle to the question, Is education a discipline? A fortiori, when the hypothesized condition does not obtain, we have no answer in principle to our question.

Let us turn finally to Mr. Scheffler's paper. He is arguing first against those who would give a case 1 answer to the question. The first two instances—the naive realist and the Platonist—are purely straw men, and Mr. Scheffler dispatches them nicely. I am not sure actually that the K + L argument works quite so well against the Platonist as it did against the naive realist. Let the Platonist hold that no truth belongs in a given discipline except that which can be deduced logically from the elemental axioms of the theory of that discipline. Let K be all truths about pure space, let L be all truth about matter in motion. The Platonist might say: "There is a theory in which all these truths may be located, but I have not the faintest idea what minimum set of axioms and definitions would do the job." Suppose we add M—all truths about the cephalic index of Andaman Islanders. The Platonist *could* hold that there is a theory in which K, L, and M could be deduced, if we but knew the appropriate axioms and definitions. This may very well be a *reductio ad absurdum* of the Platonist's view, but I am not able to see *why* it is so. If a person believed the world to be one and to be rational, he might express this belief by saying that whatever aspects or properties of the world are taken for consideration, there is at least one theory, that is, minimum set of axioms and definitions in which the truth about any set of these aspects can be deduced. He is not now disturbed about the fact the same true statement may appear in more than theory. Why should this fact disturb him? What does it prove? Merely that there are degrees of generality among theories? This would be hard to deny on any ground.

But aside from his strawmen, Mr. Scheffler's main attack is on the third, more substantial argument: because there are distinctive *terms* and *concepts* in education, education must be a discipline. This is a more substantial argument not only because it is less easily demolished but also because it more resembles what people who talk about a discipline of education have in mind.[13] The more I consider some of Mr. Scheffler's arguments here, the more puzzling I find them.

Let us take this question first: "Are there laws and theories forming a systematic body of associations that are both expressible by means of this [educational] terminology and true?" Let us assume that we are still consistent with the opening paragraph: "These questions are most serious when they refer . . . to the principle of the matter." Mr. Scheffler seems to be saying that, in principle, the answer to his question is not logical case 1; perhaps it is logical case 3, for he says the answer "is determinable, if at all, by investigation rather than by a priori arguments."

What is so puzzling? Simply this: those who seem to argue most forcibly for an autonomous discipline of education never claimed,

13. F. McMurray, "Preface to an Autonomous Discipline of Education," *Educational Theory,* V (July, 1955), 129.

so far as I know, that its existence was logically entailed by a distinctive set of educational terms. That claim would be on analysis absurd. But what would be meant by saying the question is in logical case 3 and determinable by investigation? What would we investigate? We could take every systematic theory in every science in the culture and translate each into distinctively educational terms—for "point," "line," and "plane" in Euclidean plane geometry, substitute "scope," "sequence," and "continuity" respectively. Presto! A theory of curriculum. Is it true? *That* we could investigate. Since the number of distinctive educational terms is finite and likewise the number of scientific theories in the culture, this procedure could be followed. It would be foolish and dreary to do so. But how else could we *investigate* whether, *in principle,* there are "laws and theories forming a systematic body of assertions that are both expressible in [educational] terminology and true?"

Do you say that I am being unfair, that this is not what Mr. Scheffler really meant? You are right.

There is, second, something strange in saying: "The question, Why did my new coffee table show a burn when I came back into the parlor with the cheese? is a question to which physics supplies a relevant answer." It is not strange to say that physics supplies an answer to this question. But to what or to whom would the answer be relevant? Mr. Scheffler asks me this question, for I happened to have remained uninterruptedly in the parlor with the cheese. I reply by saying that the molecular action in a certain region was increased by radiation from rapidly oxidizing organic matter, and so on. Unless I am sufficiently amusing, I shall probably give offense for being irrelevant. If I reply by saying that young Jones had one sherry too many, this answer, like the previous one, contains no explicit reference to coffee table, but it *is* relevant.

What is the point of balking here? Just this: education, like sherry parties, is a human affair of intentional and unintentional actions. The terms and concepts by which we describe and explain education are not only untheoretical because they lack systematic, logical organization, but also because they include terms and concepts that simply cannot have that sort of organization.

Mr. Scheffler says: "The terms peculiar to common affairs . . . normally figure in applying disciplines to life." We look at a weather map displaying theoretical terms and complex measurements. We ask what it means for human life. The answer comes in terms peculiar to common affairs: rain, fog, and high tides. Mr. Scheffler's description applies well here.

But suppose we are watching a classroom in session. It is not only that our descriptions of the class—what Miss Jaizen is trying to do, the responses she elicits from her pupils, the purpose of the enterprise, anything we might choose to describe—are already in terms appropriate to common affairs; the non-analogy with the weather map goes farther: some of the terms we wish to use, those that belong in the language of intention, simply could not be organized into scientific theories of any form correctly known to us. What is the purpose in teaching that? What is Miss Jaizen trying to do? Why is Timothy so quiet today? What comes after the spelling lesson? and on and on. Some of these are simply not the kind of question for which we have, are likely to have, perhaps in principle could have, theoretical answers.

You may say to yourself: That's true, but we didn't do too well with weather prediction until we got over looking at the sky anthropologically and started making purely objective measurements related by theories of fluid motion. What you say is true. But remember: the proper way to look at human behavior is anthropomorphically.

This is not to suggest, of course, that there is *no* place for theory in education nor for the language of intention in some forms of theory of human behavior. Or rather, to suggest that there is no place may be merely to encourage those who think there is a place to show what that place might be.

My second and final point: Mr. Scheffler has demonstrated to my satisfaction that the answer to his question is not logical case 1.

But then I never believed it was. Both he and those who advocate theory in education seem to believe the answer is in logical case 3. For some educational terms and concepts, this may be so. But for many it is not so.

Those who want to see the growth of educational theories are likely to speak of strategies. One of the first strategic moves would seem to be that of separating those educational terms and concepts that can be organized logically into theories, as we understand theories in science, from those that logically cannot. Who is competent and interested enough to make that move?

Is the pursuit of theory and, through theory, a discipline of education worthwhile? Not if it is logically impossible. Perhaps for most of the terms and concepts of education, the question, Is education a discipline? is best answered by showing how likely it is that the right answer is logical case 2.

IV

Education: The Discipline That Concern Built

JAMES L. KUETHE

THIS CONFERENCE on the discipline of education comes at a time
when the entire process of formal education is under a spotlight
more brilliant and more searching than ever before in history.
Never before have so many individuals been involved, so much
money been spent; and never before has there been so much doubt
about the nature and methods of education and its practitioners.
There is far less agreement today about the goals and methods of
education than there was twenty years ago. Of what is this a
symptom? Does this mean we know more? Does it mean we are
attempting to include more? Or does it simply mean that our concern has increased and as a result our doubts are greater?

It is my contention that we know quite a bit more about the
process of education, and this, together with increased concern, is
one source of the prevalent confusion. It is not my intention, if,
indeed, it is in my capacity, to go into the reasons for the increased
concern which serves to produce this confusion, or at least to give
it publicity. The challenge of conflicting ideologies in the modern
world and the staggering increase in population would no doubt
be high in the list of factors that have awakened concern. It is,
rather, my intention to argue that some degree of order can be
brought out of the chaos by the study of education as an entity in

its own right. I believe that education can be and should be studied in the same sense that the disciplines of history and physics are studied and are in turn developed through study. When I say that it is important to study education, I run the risk of being regarded as having made a statement of the quality and significance of "Love your mother" or "Let us all be loyal citizens." This is the climate of thinking at the moment in this country as a result of the publicity, favorable and unfavorable, that the educational enterprise has been receiving. It almost seems at times that the topic of education has become like classical music—many people show great interest in it because they feel they should, even if they are bored by what they hear.

I want now to come back to my statement that education should be studied. The climate is such that I could expect with almost any audience to receive vigorous nods of approval, much as if I had said we should eliminate slums. Allow me, though, to point out a quite basic assumption that I have made, an assumption easily obscured by the prevalent level of concern. My central assumption, indeed my contention, is that there is something here that can be studied. This is what I meant when I said education can and should be studied in the same sense that history or physics are studied.

It is, then, my belief that there is a developing discipline of education worthy of study in its own right. What does this mean? A discipline implies a set of teachings: at least this is the meaning of *disciplina* from where the term discipline derives. However, there is a tendency to require more of a discipline than simply that there be a set of teachings or principles. In defining a discipline many look for what might be called unique or internally developed facts and principles. This would mean unique in the sense that gravity belongs to physics and the story of 1066 is part of history.

Many will say that education is not a discipline because it does not possess a corpus of facts and principles of its own. They will perhaps say that education is an unrelated mass of borrowings, a patchwork quilt of psychology, sociology, philosophy, history, economics, and so on. If the situation were really this simple, educators would be in a position to demand of their critics, "Are you saying that what we have borrowed is wrong or are you saying that we have borrowed the wrong things?" It is hard to believe that what education has borrowed is wrong. The disciplines to which education is in debt seem quite solid and respectable. It also seems unlikely that the wrong facts and principles have been incorporated from the traditional disciplines. For many years there has been ample opportunity for empirical evaluation of principles derived elsewhere and now incorporated into the matrix of the formal education process. Many of the individuals involved in the total educational effort and its evaluation have been very capable people. Considering the magnitude of the enterprise, a very successful job has been done in this country. The United States stands out in the world as the nation that has carried the maximum benefits of education to the maximum number of its people.

It is not the possession of a unique corpus of facts that characterizes a discipline. If this were true, the disciplines of political science and economics might be hard put to demonstrate how they are more than a particular combination of psychology, sociology, statistics, and law. Disciplines can not be identified by the possession of a unique method. The methods of physics and chemistry are similar, as are the methods of psychology and sociology. If I wanted to argue that there is a discipline of education on the basis of unique concepts and practices, such things as curriculum could be stressed. If arguments were to be made on the basis of method, the idiosyncratic nature of the instructional process would receive emphasis.

Instead, I want to approach the problem from the viewpoint of concern. Education is a discipline in the sense that there is a body of facts and principles organized in a framework of a unique concern. In essence, this concern is about the transmittal of human knowledge and culture from generation to generation. Central to this concern is the involvement of society in making formal provisions for the transmission to take place. There are, of course, many crucial aspects of the education process which are not monitored by a formal system. Teachers could not start at the level they do were it not for the fact that most students have learned the rudiments of the language and the culture in their homes. Indeed, if this were not true, the entire complexion of the teacher's job would be changed. I regard the discipline of education as involving the entire educational process as its subject matter, but, of course, formal education is usually the recipient of special concern perhaps because it is most susceptible to study, and also because it is susceptible to modification by mandate.

In what way does a unique concern make itself felt in the structure of a discipline? What is unique about a discipline, I believe, is a concern with certain relations between facts. Certain relations and principles may be unique to a discipline even though they are derived from principles shared by one or more other disciplines. I would argue that concern with the economic behavior of man permits the continued existence of an independent discipline even though there is another discipline called psychology that according to its textbooks is the discipline that studies human behavior. As psychology defines its discipline it embraces economics, sociology, political science, and the languages, to name a few of the traditional subjects. Even history could, perhaps, be viewed as a chronology of behavior, or there could be a psychological approach to the understanding of history. Certainly to the extent that education is concerned with the learning process, it is concerned with something that lies within the domain staked out by psychology. These last remarks are of course the sort of things one might have expected a psychologist to say.

The increasing difficulty of drawing lines between disciplines is certainly part of the problem. I would say that biochemistry and biophysics are disciplines in their own right because of their specific concern. The fact that they appear to be manufactured out of other disciplines is not important. As a matter of fact, although I do not intend to press the point, it is possible to take the view that all of knowledge is continuously related. According to this concept all facts, all truths, are interlocking parts of some total pattern. If this is so—and it certainly is attractive to believe that it is—then any classification of knowledge into discrete disciplines is obviously arbitrary. To identify any body of knowledge and methods as a discipline would be forcing a discontinuous classification upon a continuous system.

It seems that a classification based upon unique or at least central concerns about relations is the most reasonable. Most economists are concerned with the economic behavior of people while most psychologists have specific concerns such as how people see or how they hear or how they adjust to the demands of the environment.

When many individuals have a specific concern, this concern directs their efforts, their experimentation, and their thinking. Specific concern with the process of education leads to experimentation and thinking directed at this problem. When facts, ideas, or techniques are incorporated from other areas of interest, these are taken for only one reason and this is relevance or adaptability to the problem of concern to those involved in education. I have heard Paul Tillich say that every man has a god, it is that with which he has ultimate concern. Perhaps there is the problem that concern leads to irrational involvement in a problem. This would certainly explain the utter breakdown of communication between individuals with different goals, different concerns.

At this point there is a rather obvious question that can be asked: If classification into disciplines is arbitrary, if knowledge is continuous in nature, why bother at all with the question of whether or not there is a discipline of education? Once again let us come back to the question of concern: the process of education is something that has received concern. Because we are concerned about it we shall go on studying it. Because we are concerned we shall take facts and methods from other interests to the degree to which they are of help to us in our concern.

A specific concern is a basis for the organization of principles and ideas in a unique way. In a class in educational psychology students are told how the teacher should react when a student volunteers an answer and is wrong. They are told that the teacher should inform the student that he is wrong in such a way that, while the student knows his answer was not correct, he also knows that the teacher is not angry at him and does not like him less in any way. Discussion of this point would include consideration of the manner in which this can be done. Obviously there is not going to be a scientifically exact prescription that can be given. For example, while observing at a high school, I observed a teacher handle this situation by saying, "Where is my baseball bat? I am going to bop that guy real good." The student and the class were amused but the job was done. The student knew he had been wrong but at the same time he did not feel personally rejected; he knew that the teacher would never have joked that way if he did not like him very much.

I have given this example because it serves to illustrate an important point. It embodies a principle that is, as a totality, unique to education. As a principle of formal education it might be stated: "Tell a student whether or not he is correct and, at the same time, associate this information with the student's response. Reduce as much as possible the tendency of the student to perceive such information as personal criticism." This principle is unique to education because it has to do with a process that is of concern to education. One might argue that this concept does not include anything that cannot be found in traditional psychology. It could be argued that we know from psychology that immediate knowledge of results provides the greatest efficiency of learning and this is why the teacher should bother to tell the student whether he is right or wrong in the first place. It would also be possible to find within clinical lore or in concepts of adolescent personality dynamics, information to the effect that the adolescent is especially likely to take criticism very personally and perhaps be quite disturbed.

However, nowhere in traditional psychology are these items of fact or theory combined into a unified principle in the way they are combined as a principle of education. It is quite obvious why this principle, this unique combination of fact and theory, does not occur in traditional psychology. It does not occur because it does not deal with something that is of concern to traditional psychology. The unique responsibility of education for providing for the transmittal of the culture has led to the development of this principle both from what theory has offered and results in the classroom have justified. It is the existence of a central concern that produces the body of knowledge which constitutes a discipline. In the case of education, the corpus of the discipline has several aspects: there are the direct contributions of the traditional academic disciplines, there are new formulations originating in other disciplines but modified by the specific concern of education, and there is the knowledge that has resulted directly from the practical experience of those concerned with the education enterprise. My own background in psychology causes me to emphasize that discipline when illustrating the relation between education and other areas of interest. Foundations of education in philosophy, sociology, and history will, I trust, receive more emphasis from my colleagues.

The concern of education produces selection and modification of the contributions of other disciplines on the basis of many values; dominant among them are humanitarian values. An illustration of this may be seen through the analysis of a classroom situation involving a child in conflict. Let us suppose that an animal, perhaps a raccoon, has been brought in for the children to maintain and observe. If a child is afraid to approach the animal he is placed in an approach-avoidance conflict. Out of curiosity he probably does want to approach, and it is also quite likely that the other children will exert considerable social pressure. Now if the teacher were to handle the situation on the basis of the analysis afforded by traditional psychology there would be two main alternatives: the teacher could increase the child's tendency to approach or decrease the child's tendency to avoid. Either tactic could result in the child's coming into closer contact with the animal. However, the concern of education includes consideration of developing certain valued attitudes which would be lost were the child, already motivated to approach, made more anxious. The teacher would, therefore, employ techniques for reducing the tendency to avoid— perhaps by allowing the child to become more familiar with the source of fear gradually and by indirect methods. The body of knowledge that is evolving in education is selected and unified by the total concern of education. Concern, unlike many systematic approaches to the analysis of a discipline, implies that specific values are a critical part of the framework.

These examples of the way in which knowledge from another discipline has been assimilated into the discipline of education illustrate an important point. The substances of educational theory and practice is not a crazy quilt of odds and ends from the rest of the campus. What has been taken from elsewhere has been taken only because it is relevant to the concern of education, and in almost every case this concern has produced modification of what has been incorporated.

Some have said education is philosophy, while a smaller number have claimed that it is a social science. As a discipline organized by a concern, education would be regarded as both philosophy and method. Research in education and in the traditional social sciences provides new data, new information; but it is the philosophy of education that attempts to clarify the meaning and the values these facts have.

At this point it might be mentioned that there are concepts that are completely the concern of education. One example would be theory of curriculum. However, it is not the intention of this paper to argue that education should be studied because it is capable of generating unique content. What is unique to education is its primary concern with the transmittal of the culture. Topics as diverse as the teaching of attitudes and the most effective way to illuminate the classroom are generated by this concern.

It is a serious mistake and an unfortunate loss when capable individuals come to the conclusion that there is nothing in education that can be studied. The magnitude and complexity of the education enterprise tends to obscure the existence of a central theme, namely the concern which has produced this admittedly unwieldy mass. Of course there will always be people of ability who are made anxious by confusion and the absence of precision. Some react to this by attempting to introduce order; others react by seeking areas of interest that already have considerable structure. The study of education is not going to appeal to those who are unable to tolerate considerable ambiguity.

Aspects of education have been studied by psychologists, philosophers, historians, and many other people with special orientations. It may well be that the body of knowledge that has evolved in education can produce a new generation of scholars. These would be scholars of education, men who would regard education as their discipline, not merely as the name of their department or as a collection of method courses. These second-generation scholars will be concerned with all aspects of the transmittal of the culture, an endeavor as valid and at least as worthy as the study of the traditional social sciences. These will not be people whose primary goal is to improve their own skill as instructors; there will be relatively more emphasis on studying education because it itself is a challenging area of knowledge. These scholars might even be similar in sentiment to the pure mathematician who considers the possibility of practical application an inadequate justification of his interest. It is quite possible that these scholars will not think of themselves as educators; that label already has too many connotations and the connotations are not all favorable. These men will be a different breed from most people now referred to as educators, and the term would perhaps be an unfortunate handicap to inflict upon them. A different label does not come readily to mind, at least not one that is neither cumbersome nor pretentious.

On the other hand, it might be well if such people remained identified clearly with education; the public image of education might be upgraded as a result. Education at the moment does have renewed status, not because we have suddenly done better but as a result of both international developments and the changing basis for evaluating personal status in this culture. Education has become related to personal status somewhat by default. Family background has become an unreliable criterion now that families have become scattered, and money gives less status than it once did because of the decreased variability of the population's buying power.

When the hucksters of Madison Avenue use educators as a status symbol to sell cigarettes, it is evident that the climate has changed. True scholars of education are in a better position to receive moral and financial support than they have been for some time. There is the possibility of a bright future for the discipline if the new breed can avoid insulting the intelligent with nonsense and can restrain itself from generating the jargon which has encouraged ridicule in the past.

Some may feel that concern with transmittal of the culture involves many facets of our society that go beyond the proper boundaries of any discipline of education. There are those who would limit their concern to the formal or institutionalized provisions that society has set up for the instruction of its citizens. It might be argued by the advocates of this position that, even with this restriction, the diversity of topics included, ranging from constitutional law to audio-visual aids, prohibits the unification of concepts required for a discipline. Once again I would emphasize the view that the central concern of education is the source of unity and the basis for the study of the discipline.

The learning that occurs in the home, on the streets, and in the motion-picture houses is an essential part of the transmittal of the culture. It would not be a difficult task to argue that the real substance of the culture, the most important attitudes and response predispositions, are acquired outside of the classroom. Perhaps it is because people are little and inadequate when they start school and large and articulate when they emerge that the schools get some credit, as well as blame, that is not completely deserved. It certainly is true that the nature of formal education should be determined by what it can assume is learned elsewhere as well as by the instruction that it feels to be its particular responsibility. For example, if the school could not assume that most of the students already had the basic rudiments of the language, the type of activities carried on the first years would be quite different. The fact that the teacher can communicate to a moderate extent with beginning elementary students makes possible the method of instruction usually employed. If the schools had to start at a different level, they would; in fact this is what occurs in some cases. What this means is that the schools should not be committed to teaching what they do in the way they do; the important thing is that there is a goal. The schools cannot rigidly identify themselves with a particular part of the job that must be done; the schools must respond to the total concern. Those entrusted with providing formal education can only respond to the total concern of education through a comprehension of the total process of education. It is the formal system that is in a position to perceive what is lacking, what part of the culture is inadequately transmitted elsewhere, and to dedicate the large part of its effort toward completing the aim of education.

Where do we go from here? If we accept the existence of a discipline of education based on a central concern and guided in its development by the ramifications of this concern, would not scholars of education be mere monitors of the process? The answer is of course, No. The foreman knows that he must supervise the production of an automobile, but the process of education does not produce such an objective result. In the factory the specifications of the end product are agreed upon before work begins; in education there has been very little consideration of the ultimate goal. To the extent goals are verbalized, one hears "Children need algebra" or "The colleges require us to give two years of a language."

Lack of a unified approach to carefully considered goals results in waste that can no longer be afforded. A student in high school in the eleventh grade will take a chemistry course in which he is required to memorize the valences of the common elements. One year later most of this information is forgotten. The following year the student memorizes the valences again as part of his college freshman chemistry course. Three years later when he is receiving his degree from the department of Romance Languages he will have forgotten the chemical valences a second time. Perhaps it is not really disastrous that he has twice learned and forgotten this information, for no one will ever notice!

The study of education can lead to clarification of the concern of education. The question of what things are worth teaching lacks systematic consideration. Perhaps the now popular attempts to program instruction will force a partial answer to this problem. When material is programmed, the requirements of continuity and relatedness force the programmer to concentrate on where he is headed as well as what he is presenting at a given moment. This is a consideration lacking in many textbooks and most lectures with the result that often the student does not actually know what it is that he should learn. The importance of letting the student know what he should learn is, of course, another basic principle of education.

The teaching of attitudes remains on a hit-or-miss basis even though attitudes toward the education process acquired by students in elementary school are crucial in shaping future progress. Study of the culture and the process by which it is transmitted is fundamental to full consideration of this problem. What attitudes should be taught and the optimum way in which to teach them is another topic that needs systematic study.

These questions and many others are basic to the aims of education. Principles of transmitting the culture are principles of education. Only scholars who share the concern of education will be able to develop these principles and integrate them into the discipline of education. But the rigorous study of education will proceed, for the concern about education and its relations will demand proof and explanation.

COMMENTS   *Edward Joseph Shoben, Jr.*

A primary question that cannot be avoided in any consideration of education as a discipline is that of whether it matters how we classify the educational enterprise. A second query, posed by Dr. Kuethe's well-reasoned argument, has to do with whether a discipline can be built by public concern.

Perhaps we can generate some useful responses to these issues and enlarge in some small degree our understanding of education as a serious human activity by contrasting a *discipline* with a *profession*. There is no intention here of dwelling on the precise and elaborate definitions so dear to the logician. All that is sought is some general sense of the differences between two categories as a basis for exploring their implications.

To begin with, it seems accurate to characterize a discipline as an intellectual venture that derives its value from adding to knowledge, resynthesizing knowledge, or developing new methods of studying or interpreting some definable domain of inquiry. A profession, on the other hand, is essentially an activity that derives its value from the character of the services it provides to society at large or to some significant segment of it. To suggest that a discipline and a profession differ in their primary sources of value is *not* to assert that there are no ways or occasions when they share or overlap in the functions for which they are prized. We are concerned only with the general rule, not the exceptions that impose restrictions upon it; and in general, it seems reasonably clear that the disciplines are *fundamentally* judged by their discoveries or reinterpretations of knowledge, the professions by the quality and types of services that they make available.

Second, the internal affairs of a discipline—the conduct of its practitioners, the circulation of information relevant to its concerns, the determination of qualifications for practice—are regulated in a more or less individualistic way and with considerable variation almost entirely by the discipline's own representatives. A primary device for such regulation is the learned society. Free of preoccupations with such matters as codes of ethics, jurisdictional disputes over the appropriate functions of its members in relation to those of some other discipline, or the legislation of differential training standards, the learned society is typically devoted to the facilitation and dissemination *within its own discipline* of scholarship. Again, the learned society may certainly become involved in other matters, but its principal business is usually concerned with publication, the advancement of scholarly activity, and the clarification of substantive issues in its own field. In any case, the learned society as the organizational manifestation of a discipline is basically answerable only to its own members.

With respect to a profession, the organizational picture is rather different. The professional association may deal with substantive problems and occupy itself with the advancement of research and scholarship, but it *must* direct its primary attention to other matters. As Carr-Saunders and Wilson [1] have pointed out, although a learned society may be helpful to a discipline, formal association is essential to a profession, which is responsible, both collectively and in the individual persons of its members, to society and must therefore maintain formal channels of communication with society's decision-making bodies, such as legislatures, the press, and civic leaders. Thus, one of the basic functions of the professional association is the protection it gives to the individual practitioners who compose it and the heightened power it is able to wield on their behalf through its institutional character.

But, as Tawney [2] and others have suggested, an overemphasis on these protective and self-aggrandizing activities may weaken the

1. A. M. Carr-Saunders and P. A. Wilson, *The Professions* (New York: Oxford University Press, 1933).

2. R. H. Tawney, *The Acquisitive Society* (New York: Harcourt, Brace and Howe, 1920).

professional organization and threaten the status of the profession itself. An important aspect of a profession's corporate business then becomes the curbing of selfish or opportunistic behavior among its practitioners. Taeusch [3] has argued that this objective is most effectively approximated through the tabus informally imposed by the group, but the fact remains that virtually all professions have written codes of ethics, generated, prepared, and administered through their associations. By means of a police power foreign to the learned society, professional associations may censure or expel members who transgress the code, actions which usually have serious consequences for the livelihood and status of the individuals involved.

In this tension between the protective and the police powers of the professional association, one finds at least the source of the most distinctive criterion of a profession. Flexner [4] stated it most emphatically when he insisted that the differentiating hallmark of the professions is their altruism, their devotion to the interests of others, and their denial of the egoistic spirit. In principle, the self-aggrandizing efforts of professional bodies are directed at increasing the quality and worth of the services they are called upon to provide; and, conversely, the policing function is exercised to insure adequate adherence to the standards of responsibility and altruism that those services entail.

We need not blind ourselves to the other side of this coin to recognize its currency. There is no doubt that the professions are a means of livelihood and financial reward, nor can we escape the question of whether the sharp restrictions a profession sometimes imposes on the number of people admitted to it often work a hardship on the public it presumably serves. Nevertheless, as Parsons [5] has made clear, although the distinction between altruism and

3. C. F. Taeusch, *Professional and Business Ethics* (New York: Henry Holt, 1926).

4. A. Flexner, "Is Social Work a Profession?" *School and Society,* I (1915), 901–11.

5. T. Parsons, *Essays in Sociological Theory* (Glencoe, Ill.: Free Press, 1945).

egoism may break down when applied to professionals and others as individuals, the *institutional* situation of the professions is such as to instigate a greater degree of altruistic behavior and a more marked service orientation than is the case with business or the trades. With respect to the disciplines, the case seems to hold reasonably well. The behavior of a physician, for example, must be appropriately responsive in some significant degree to the needs of his patients, regardless of his own convenience or profit. The behavior of a physiologist, on the other hand, need have no relevance whatsoever to the urgencies of a specified clientele. The identification of similar analogies between other basic disciplines and the professions that draw upon them for advancements in knowledge would not be difficult, and the emphasis on "pure" research, so typically and properly prized among the disciplines, sets them apart from the professions and their stress on application, utility in service contexts, and "practicality." If both the disciplines and the professions require an extensive intellectual training and are founded on theories about the nature of things, the way in which these overlapping backgrounds are put to work seems quite different, and the difference is clarified if we regard it as distributed over such continua as altruistic-egoistic or pure-applied, especially if we can divest ourselves—not an easy job—of the pejorative connotations of these terms.

Perhaps the most common and probably the most effective method by which a profession maintains its tradition of public responsibility and its stress on the quality of service—including, of course, the development of skills and knowledge as well as of attitude and orientation—is the relatively strict regulation of membership. As Ulich says, ". . . the consolidation of a profession . . . goes hand in hand with the establishment of standards and entrance requirements . . . historical studies of professions and their preparations point to the fact that without a definite formalism and rigidity in the procedure of selection and appointment, corruption and decay are bound to occur." [6]

6. R. Ulich, *Crisis and Hope in American Education* (Boston: Beacon Press, 1951).

Professional status, unfortunately, seems to be purchased only at the cost of relatively inflexible rules that at times are likely to work hardships on individuals and even on the general populace. Nevertheless, professional service seems most efficiently implemented through enforced standards of selection and training that are more formalized and less subject to experimentation than is the case with the disciplines. We are not concerned with whether the admissions standards or training programs for medicine or law are higher or more difficult than those for careers in biological or behavioral science. We *are* concerned with the degree of formalization associated with them.

One reason for this differential degree of formalization is the immediate stake that society has in the functioning of the professions as against its relative indifference to the disciplines. The admission to their various practices of physicians, lawyers, engineers, and teachers is a matter in which the state takes an active interest through the mechanism of licensing or certification and its attendant regulation of training. Physiologists, psychologists, and physicists, on the other hand, may go their disciplinary way undisturbed by the state until their discoveries or newly developed skills acquire professional—that is, service or applied—significance. Thus, the translation of atomic theory into available nuclear energy has thrown physicists into a not entirely comfortable partnership with the profession of the military and has brought into being an infant profession of nuclear engineering. Similarly, psychology has undergone a turbulent development since World War II by virtue of the responsiveness of a part of its membership to the mental health needs of the United States. While the growth of clinical psychology has been uneven and has entailed severe stresses within the psychological discipline, it seems clear that it has established itself on a genuinely professional footing—witness the state certification laws, the codes of ethics, and the standardization of admissions and training patterns that have come into being with it.

Two points are worth making in relation to this societal stake in the conduct of a profession. First, it means that a profession acquires a certain degree of political power, either by achieving statutory recognition and a share in state-administered regulatory authority or by an ability, at least partially won because of the worth of the services provided, to influence public opinion. Quite apart from any psychological drives for power or recognition that may be involved, this entry into the political arena seems necessary because legal, legislative, and social conditions bear upon the efficiency with which a profession may render its services. Some segment of a profession, then, must attend to legislative trends, the dissemination of information about the profession to its consuming public, its relations with other professions, and so on. Except for the issue of academic freedom, the members of a discipline are rarely affected by such matters and typically pride themselves on their lack of involvement.

Second, the converse of this point also holds. Because society has a direct and immediate concern with professional activities, it requires the professions to submit to a degree of regulation from outside themselves. The official representatives of the society—legislators, public administrators, and elected officials—have a significant say in the licensing and the general conditions of practice of medicine, law, teaching, architecture, and so forth. Because of their altruistic purposes and their service orientation, the professions can only accept a certain amount of this overseeing from outside their own ranks as correct within the structure of organized society. The disciplines, by contrast, are quite properly inclined to resent any such interference by societal officialdom in their research of thought. In short, the disciplines operate in a realm where, if they are to be productive, society must grant full freedom for the scholar to pursue any line of reasoning or investigation to whatever terminus it may lead. The professions, on the other hand, engage in services that society is expected both to facilitate and to buy. If this expectancy is to be fulfilled, then it is reasonable also to expect that society will reserve the right to criticize and regulate them to a far greater degree than it does the disciplines, from which it is much farther removed and which serve very different functions.

These observations suggest that education is much more susceptible to classification as a profession than as a discipline, and some important questions are raised about Dr. Kuethe's interesting presentation. For example, his basic contention is that education is a discipline because its facts and principles are "organized in a framework by the existence of a unique concern." It seems hard to deny that this statement is also applicable to medicine and engineering—or, for that matter, to plumbing and business administration. Is it also applicable to literary scholarship, psychology, or chemistry? It appears improbable. The facts, the principles, and the methods of the literary scholar can be animated by little more than a concern for the establishment of a given text, the identification of its sources, or the analysis in some terms of the themes it may have in common with other texts. In other words, to the extent that his concern is especially relevant, it is given by his evaluation of the traditions of his discipline. It neither defines nor creates that discipline.

But perhaps Dr. Kuethe means the concerns of society at large, not those of particular practitioners. If such is the case, it is noteworthy that the concern he speaks of is the "concern with the transmittal of human knowledge and culture from generation to generation." We can have no quarrel with this function of transmission as a central part of the total educative process, but does it define a discipline? After all, it is precisely this concern that calls the institution of the family into being; and while none of us would be content to classify parenthood as a discipline, it would qualify reasonably well, except for the requirement of extensive intellectual training and a foundation in theories about the nature of things, for what we have functionally defined as a profession. Parenthood is necessarily service oriented, entails institutionally a degree of altruism, is subject to many kinds of state regulation, and acquires some measure of political power, as any student of school bond elections knows. Although it is something of a *reductio ad absurdum,* this example suggests that a widespread public concern— like that for redressing insults to bodily tissues or reversing disease processes—may play a significant role in the creation of a profession; it seems unlikely to have a major or even a distinctive part in the defining of a domain of knowledge to be enlarged for its own sake.

This brings us to Dr. Kuethe's central assumption that in education "there is something that can be studied . . . in the same sense that history or physics are studied." None of us will disagree that some process called education is susceptible to investigation and reflection. But what are we talking about, and what is the significance of that crucial clause, "in the same sense that history or physics are studied"? If we mean to equate education and the entire socialization process, a notion that would be congenial to some of us, then it is obvious that psychologists, anthropologists, and sociologists have for a long time regarded socialization as a part of their own overlapping territories of inquiry. Freud, for example, was much preoccupied with the shaping impact of childhood experience on adult character and behavior and spoke quite explicitly about the educative quality of the conflict between the fundamental instincts and the restrictive, nay-saying environment. But if psychoanalysis is relevant for education, it is hardly a synonym for it, and the business of education seems to be far more the professional application of Freudian or other systematic theories of socialization than that of laying claim to socialization as a field of pure inquiry.

If, on the other hand, we restrict ourselves to what occurs or should occur in the school as an institution, then we also encounter trouble with Dr. Kuethe's formulation. If we attend to questions of how the experience of school ought to affect the development of individual children or the character of the state, we are behaving like philosophers, dealing with old but ever-new issues having to do with the ideal man or the good society. Should we turn to matters of the conditions under which learning most effectively takes place, we are assuming the role of psychologists, studying the nature and conditions of learning. If we ask about the structures and functions of schools under various social and governmental patterns, then we don the mantle of the sociologist or the anthropologist, interested in the comparative ways in which various parts of culture relate to each other and to the whole. Likewise, if we grow curious about the processes of change over time in the structure of the school as an institution or in methods of instruction, then we take on the historian's guise and, if we are responsible, subject ourselves to the discipline of his methods and work within the framework of his other facts and principles that have relevance for our particular interest.

The point, of course, is obvious. As an object of study, education lies across a number of disciplines and may be profitably examined from many disciplinary angles of regard. Just as one may legitimately and usefully investigate the ethics of the business community, the sociology of medicine, the history of football, or the psychology of prostitution, so one may legitimately and usefully study the ethics, the sociology, the history, or the psychology of education. This fact does not in itself, however, make business, medicine, football, prostitution, or education into a discipline. It only demonstrates that the special stance of the disciplines may be taken with enlightenment toward various forms of occupational behavior and their moral, social, or other implications. The fact that education can be studied is irrelevant to its possible status as a discipline, and that it can be studied from the point of view of so many different disciplines suggests that it is markedly different from history or physics.

But what does it matter? Why should anyone care whether we call education a discipline, a profession, or something else? At least a relevant answer lies in the nature of the relationship between a profession and the disciplines related to it. A brief examination of this relationship may repay our attention.

It will be remembered that a profession is primarily devoted to human service, a discipline to rolling back the boundaries of some definable domain of knowledge; both entail extensive intellectual training and a grounding in theory. A profession, then, comes into being to assist in men's efforts to cope with particular kinds of often poignant and frequently crucial problems that must be solved if the texture of life is to acquire a more engaging quality. But while a profession must thus be actively involved in practicalities of great immediacy and direct human importance, its basis in theory permits it to formulate these practical problems in intellectual terms. In consequence, professional practice becomes a rich source of issues for consideration by the disciplines. The profession of psychiatry provides a good example. From the clinical experience of the psychiatrist can be formulated questions which properly demand the attention of the neurophysiologist and the biochemist in their attack on the ignorance that surrounds our knowledge of how brain processes affect behavior, of the psychologist in his effort to understand more fully the relationship of earlier experience to later performance and the laws of development and learning, of the sociologist in his preoccupation with clarifying the interplay between social structures and the deviant behavior of individuals, and of the moral philosopher in his enterprise of defining the characteristics of the good life. This infusion of problems formulated from the experience of those practical and urgent difficulties that are the business of the professions enriches the disciplines and enlarges their horizons. Much of the impetus to seventeenth-century physics came from the new problems attendant upon the development of artillery, and the enormous expansion of psychological research in the decade of the fifties was touched off by America's mental health problems and the necessary growth of the clinical professions.

Conversely, if the disciplines draw upon professional experience for new and invigorating problems, the disciplines provide the professions with the basic knowledge, including many of the reformulated or novel ideas, on which they must depend. To provide services that keep pace with human needs in a rapidly changing world, the professions require constant transfusions of new information, new ways of regarding their fields of practice, and new notions of how their particular classes of human problems can best be dealt with. The disciplines provide this reservoir of fresh perspectives and knowledge upon which effective professional service relies. Perhaps one of the most dramatic examples of this reliance is the extent to which the Supreme Court leaned on the opinions of behavioral scientists in arriving at its 1954 decision with respect to school desegregation.

True enough, this reciprocal dependency between the professions and the disciplines is not without its tensions. The professional, often desperate to find some way of coping with the urgent difficulties of his clientele, is very often liable to the charge of acting on the basis of grossly inadequate evidence or of being a naive empiricist who responds to the expedient or perpetuates a private mystique of well-intentioned but ill-grounded service. The member of a discipline, on the other hand, is with equal frequency vulnerable to attack because of his lack of responsiveness to human need and his coolly removed approach to the investigation of nature for its own sake, an idea which lends itself easily to mistranslation as "for the pleasure of the investigator." Such outbreaks of temper and misunderstanding are probably consequences of the different but symbiotic orientations that the disciplines and professions take toward their obligations and of the character of those obligations themselves. Uncomfortable as they are at times, they probably reflect nothing more than another instance of the law that nothing can be had without a price; and the mutually supportive roles that the disciplines and the professions play in relation to each other seem to entail this kind of cost.

It seems likely that the cost could be somewhat reduced, however, if the professions and the disciplines understood one another a bit better. Nowhere is this possibility more apparent than in education and its relationships to the several disciplines that have relevance for it. It has become a cliché to say that few enterprises of the modern age are so important as education. If our schools and colleges are to do their jobs well—indeed, if they are to identify those jobs in workable and useful terms at all—they will need a stock of ideas and knowledge that it will tax the disciplines to supply. Yet without such resources as some of our best philosophical thinking devoted to educational issues and some of our best psychological efforts invested in a clarifying of the human learning process under actual field conditions, it is quite possible that we will fail. Put the other way around, much of the success of the educational enterprise may depend on an increased responsiveness among the disciplines to the problems perceived and initially formulated by the professionals, those who work directly and under conditions of social responsibility with the actual organization and administration of schools, the development of curricula, and the teaching of youngsters.

Perhaps one way of achieving this deeper and more understanding levy by the profession of education on the various disciplines of inquiry, on the one hand, and, on the other, a greater responsiveness among the disciplines to professionally identified social needs is through the development of persons who are both educators and members of a discipline. The physician who is also a biochemist is no longer a *rara avis* in medicine and the health sciences. Jurisprudence has always been a route by which lawyers could become formally involved in the behavioral sciences or their forerunners or in social philosophy. Clinical psychology represents a unique—and, so far, essentially successful—effort to build a profession that retains disciplinary roots and requires at least some of its members to be scientists as well as practitioners. The "foundation movement" in education, which held this kind of potentiality within it, never seemed to pursue such a goal in any articulate fashion. Rather, it was primarily an effort to acquaint professionals with the basic disciplines upon which they could draw without developing either the loyalties or the skills of the career student, where career studentship is simply another name for systematic problem-solving within a special domain of investigation and thought.

Education could benefit from greater numbers of practitioner-scholars, both because of the special contributions such people could make and because of the bridge they would provide across the sometimes disturbingly wide chasm that separates the professional educator from the disciplines that are centrally relevant for him. If the strategy of producing such new explorers of the educational frontiers is to be employed, however, it is important that the different functions of the professions and the disciplines be kept clear and comprehensible. Confusions are liable to distort the relatively delicate relationship between the two, the character of the distinctive job of each, and the task of harmonizing two essential roles, whether that task is undertaken by men trained in both or by a different and creative organization of those representing the profession and those representing the disciplines.

PART TWO

The Relation of Education
to Other Academic Disciplines

V

The Place of Educational Psychology in the Study of Education

JOHN B. CARROLL

The inquiry to which this conference is addressed involves a difficult terminological question. If I may venture a prediction, the discussion will revert a number of times to the problem of what, exactly, we mean when we characterize something as a discipline. What would be meant by saying that education is a discipline? For that matter, what would be meant if somebody claimed that education is not a discipline? Etymologically, there is little problem; the word derives from Latin *disciplina,* instruction, education, learning and of course ultimately from *discere,* to learn. The Romans used the word *disciplina* both as a generic term for instruction and also as a term referring to any branch of knowledge, such as history or philosophy. Even in Roman times, however, the word seems also to have acquired the connotation, "the following of rigid rules." It was used to refer to the severity of military training and to the harsh but beneficial teachings of adversity. In contrast, the positive and liberalizing aspects of knowledge and learning were embodied in the Latin term *scientia,* from which we derive our word science. But during the two millennia since Roman times the meaning of the word science has wandered off to become most closely identified with those branches of learning which deal with natural phenomena. The ancient Romans were perfectly content to use the term *scientia* in referring to philosophy and history; we in contemporary times, however, are prone to use the word discipline for these branches of learning, because we hesitate to call them sciences. This usage carries the lurking implication that these branches of learning have disciplinary value—that the harsh rules they bid us to follow will strengthen our minds, our characters, or both. No such implication is necessary. Perhaps we have here a good example of the way in which words confuse our thinking. If so, in the present case we can blame the Romans! The purpose of this etymological excursion, in any event, is to draw attention to the connotational booby traps which are implicit in the term discipline, and also to point out its relation to the term science, which we shall be using later.

It must be that there is an ellipsis in our title, *The Discipline of Education*. Education itself is essentially a process, not a branch of learning or a discipline. The *study* of education may, however, be regarded as a branch of learning. The question of whether the study of education may be regarded also as a discipline cannot be resolved until we can come to agreement concerning the meaning of this term.

In order to do so, at least to a first approximation, let us sketch some of the common properties of the various branches of learning, including the disciplines (as we are accustomed to call such branches as philosophy, mathematics, history, or jurisprudence) and the sciences (such as physics, biology, and psychology).

First of all, let us note that each of these branches of learning studies some sector of the total range of phenomena with which men concern themselves, and that each study must have some distinct way of defining the sector to which it addresses itself. The story of how these sectors have become divided off, and how they have merged and divided again, is a matter for the philosopher and the historian of science; we cannot develop it here. We must point out, however, that even within any one branch of learning there are specialties and subspecialties. One specialty in biology is genetics, and a subspecialty is the genetics of the fruit-fly; one specialty in psychology is animal psychology, and a subspecialty is the psychology of the white rat.

A second characteristic of each branch of learning is that the knowledge it contains is in some way *structured*. One of the most exciting events in the intellectual experience of a bright child as he develops is the discovery that knowledge can have structure. This discovery may come about in many ways, for example, in the discovery that it makes a difference how things are sorted, that concepts and categories can be mutually exclusive, and that knowledge of one concept is prerequisite to the learning of another. Children perceive quickly that some branches of learning are characteristically more structured than others: that English language study is more structured than the study of history, for example, but that the study of mathematics is most highly structured. Many students thirst for structure in knowledge and are uncomfortable in a subject like English literature, where opinions and judgments seem to be unpatterned and unpredictable even if polarized. Often, students who have been successful with Euclidean geometry express the wish that other subjects could be taught with the same kind of order and logic. Students who pursue their intellectual quest into college and beyond come to realize that the finding of structure, order, and regularity in any subject matter is the essential goal of any intellectual activity, and that this can be done not only in disciplines like mathematics, logic, and the natural sciences, but also —although in a different way—in the humanistic disciplines and in disciplines like law, public administration, and business.

Let us say, then, that it is true of every discipline that at least some parts of its subject matter are characterized by what we can call structure, order, and regularity, and that it is the hope of those who follow a discipline that their subject matter can be more and more exhaustively described in this way. Some disciplines are highly developed in their capacity to state findings in terms of generalized propositions or laws, often employing logical or quantitative procedures in so doing. Other disciplines are not as highly developed in this respect, but may instead be highly developed in the completeness and detail with which they can describe a range of phenomena.

A third characteristic of every discipline is that it possesses a recognized set of heuristic procedures for gaining new knowledge and, usually, a set of procedures for structuring and ordering the knowledge already gained. The natural sciences have their experimental and observational methods; the social sciences have their field methods; the humanities have their historical and bibliographical methods. Mathematics is widely used for structuring and analyzing new knowledge, but this is by no means the only method. Theory construction, hypothesis-testing, and even sheer classification are valid heuristic methods.

It is probably characteristic of each branch of learning, even one like philosophy, that it intends some kind of utility in practical affairs. For those where the utilitarian aspect is strongly developed —such as law, medicine, chemistry, mechanical engineering—it is the case that they offer more or less *standardized* measuring devices, tools, and techniques for use in the application of their findings to the solution of specific practical problems or for the treatment of individual cases. For example, medical science has developed a tremendous armamentarium of drugs and devices for diagnosing and treating bodily ills. Even a discipline like history can offer a series of techniques for solving a problem like the settling of an American Indian claim.

Thus, we have four criteria for identifying a discipline:

(1) A specifiable scope of inquiry
(2) The possession of structured subject-matter
(3) A recognized set of procedures for gaining new knowledge (including criteria for stating the validity of new knowledge), and a set of procedures for ordering new knowledge
(4) Accepted techniques and tools for applying knowledge in specific cases to specified practical ends

One may make an offhand guess that the study of education meets the four criteria I have stated. Its scope of inquiry is the conduct of education and training, wherever it may occur; it possesses a considerable body of structured subject matter—classified along such dimensions as time, geography, level of education, purpose of the curriculum, and so on; it possesses, at least in some of its branches, accepted sets of procedures for gaining and verifying new knowledge; and it possesses well-recognized techniques for applying knowledge in specific cases. But it is not my intention to support this guess beyond this preliminary stage; it can remain for others to decide whether the study of education as a whole meets these criteria.

I take it that we will be in a better position to decide whether education is a discipline after we have considered the status of a number of branches of learning or investigation that are often subsumed under the study of education, or that are ancillary to this study. One of these branches of learning is educational psychology, and it will be my task in the remainder of this essay to analyze its status as a discipline and as a specialty aiding the study of education.

Educational psychology is usually regarded as an applied science, a part of psychology just as abnormal psychology and industrial psychology are parts of psychology. The demonstration that educational psychology is also a discipline which meets the four criteria stated above should be rather easy. Nevertheless, it may be of disciplinary value to proceed through this demonstration. We must, after all, recognize that there has been in the past a good deal of skepticism, possibly justified, about the status and prospects of educational psychology. Perhaps we can find some of the reasons for this skepticism.

1. *The scope and aims of educational psychology.*—The question of the scope of educational psychology is an extremely important one. We shall be more inclined to view educational psychology as a discipline if we can define its scope. As a practical matter, the way we define this scope will influence our decisions respecting the training of educational psychologists and the training of teachers in educational psychology.

The scope of educational psychology as an applied science might be regarded as practically coterminous with that of psychology itself. This is true for at least two reasons. There is hardly any aspect of the whole field of psychology which could not conceivably be brought into play in some educational problem, because the enterprise of education is concerned with many kinds of people—of different ages, degrees of ability and drive, and kinds of personality—as well as with many kinds of subject matter and skills. The description, analysis, and prediction of such diverse forms of behavior as may be encountered in education could demand findings, principles, and techniques from almost any phase of psychological science. Secondly, it can be claimed that the concept which unifies all psychology, and which is its central concern, is *learning*. Obviously, learning is the concern of education.

Educational psychologists would hardly care to bargain for all the trouble psychologists have had in defining the science of psychology. If psychologists try to identify *behavior* as the object of their concern, they must be prepared to differentiate their interest from that of the economist, who studies economic behavior; the lawyer, who is concerned with legal behavior; or even the mathematician, who might be said to study mathematical behavior. And there has long been a question as to the degree to which the psychologist interested in sense perception is poaching on the territory of the sensory physiologist. Nevertheless, psychologists have been able to come to terms with the problem of defining their science by constructing definitions which refer to the generalized properties of organismic behavior in relation to the characteristics of the organism itself and to the environment. Educational psychologists can rest content with these definitions as far as psychology proper is concerned. Educational psychology is the study of the behavioral properties of human organisms which may have to be taken into account in the management of learning and other behavior in educational settings if certain specified objectives are to be attained. In pursuing this study, the educational psychologist may draw upon techniques and results from any branch of psychology, including, for example, comparative psychology. Education ordinarily concerns only certain standard techniques for modifying behavior, such as the use of verbal and graphic communication, but the educational psychologist may wish to take cognizance of abnormal ways of modifying behavior, such as hypnosis and brainwashing, either to consider their possible usefulness or to provide protection against them.

From the fact that educational psychology may reach into almost any field of general psychology, it does not follow that every scientific problem in psychology is necessarily of interest to educational psychology. The *Journal of Educational Psychology* could hardly open its pages to contributions from *any* phase at all of psychology. The criterion of immediate or potential significance for the conduct of education would have to be applied. For example, a study of visual acuity would not normally be admissible, but other things being equal, if it included a study of the perception of typefaces by school children, it might be highly relevant to the choice or design of textbooks for the school and could be accepted for publication. There is a continuous spectrum of scientific concerns ranging from those which are highly general and of little specific interest to education to those which are centrally positioned in the area of educational psychology.

Still, there are problems in selecting and treating material for educational psychology textbooks. To what extent should one include, in an ideal textbook or treatise on educational psychology, the topics on sensory psychology, perception, reaction time, emotion, and mental mechanisms which are standard fare in general psychology texts? Educational psychology texts tend to exclude consideration of these matters; a casual search has disclosed only one contemporary educational psychological textbook [1] which attempts to cover general principles of psychology including the topics mentioned here. But most educational psychology texts are written for teachers and prospective teachers, rather than for

1. William C. Morse and G. Max Wingo, *Psychology and Teaching* (Chicago: Scott, Foresman and Co., 1955).

prospective educational psychologists; because it may be difficult to convince teachers of the relevance of certain materials from experimental psychology, these materials are omitted. Yet I would claim that a specialist in educational psychology should have a substantial acquaintance with various branches of experimental psychology, because the learner's behavior is dependent upon many characteristics of stimuli both seen and heard. The educational psychologist must know something about these characteristics— how they affect behavior and how they can be studied. Similar arguments can be made to support the proposition that the educational psychologist should be well acquainted with methods, theories, and findings in social, abnormal, and clinical psychology. Indeed, he must be as much of a generalist as he can afford to be, but he will have to go far beyond the current textbooks in order to become one. There is need for truly professional textbooks in this field which will interpret the total range of material in psychology for its educational implications.

In seeking to expand the usual concept of the scope of educational psychology, I take it for granted that human learning and human development in all of their phases are of central concern. The modern study of learning developed, in the hands of E. L. Thorndike, in an educational setting. Apart from their value in pure science, findings about learning, if they are to have any application at all, have their principal application *in education,* and it is of significance that many psychologists who are in the forefront in the study of learning—for example, Guthrie, Hilgard, Skinner, and Bruner—have indeed worked on problems of education.

Despite the great overlap between the subject matter of educational psychology and that of psychology in general, it will keep matters straight to distinguish the two fields—psychology as a pure science of behavior with no obligation to concern itself with practical applications, and educational psychology as an applied science of behavior in educational settings which possesses the moral imperative to produce knowledge and technology that will be useful in those settings. This distinction is in large measure only theoretical. It is pointless to concern oneself with the degree to which the day-to-day work of the psychologist, pure or applied, is oriented toward pure science or toward application. Attempts to apply theories in practical settings often lead to useful extensions or modifications of those theories, and even the purest of theories may suddenly be seen to have some unexpected practical utility.

A statement of the scope of educational psychology should also mention its aims. Two kinds of objectives can be spelled out for this science. First, it aims to be useful in providing part of the research background which is needed to formulate educational policy, educational policy being understood to concern itself with such questions as who should be educated, when and at what ages the various parts of the curriculum should be presented, and what kinds of education should be provided for different groups of potential students. Secondly, educational psychology can provide knowledge and tools that are of value in the practice of education. The tools and techniques of measurement and diagnosis developed in educational psychology have obviously had a widespread acceptance and influence. There is reason to hope that generalizations and principles derived from the study of learning, perception, and cognition will have an increasing impact upon the preparation of learning materials, upon the training of teachers, and upon the conduct of the classroom.

2. *The structure of the subject matter of educational psychology.*—To what extent does the content of educational psychology present itself as structured, ordered, and lawful? In approaching this question, as with the previous question, we find that we must answer not only for educational psychology but also for the broader field of psychology. And there we find a puzzling, though somewhat hopeful picture—puzzling because of the fact that resolution has by no means been found among the many systematic positions that have been proposed and hopeful because of the success that has thus far been achieved in developing and testing postulational systems. Hull's system remains an unfinished monument to its shaper. The mathematical learning theories of Bush, Mosteller, Estes, and

others [2] are as yet too limited in scope to be regarded as general postulational systems. Skinner's efforts towards building a comprehensive description of behavior [3] are buttressed at least as much by *a priori* speculation as by experimental data. There are certain bright spots within the field of psychometrics where a set of postulates can carry us a decent way along the road to a complete theory of the limited set of behavior we call test-item responses, for example, Thurstone's development of test theory,[4] and Lord's more recent development of a theory of test scores.[5] In the main, however, psychology continues to be an aggregation of small-scale, limited-focus theories, plus a multitude of loosely related empirical facts. It is not yet possible to write a treatise in psychology with the operational rigor and sequence of a subject like physics. Even if it were, one doubts that a highly quantified psychological system would be of any help to teachers, although it might indeed be useful to educational psychologists in formulating experiments or planning educational programs.

What we have in psychology today is a useful set of concepts and a series of reasonably well-attested empirical laws. For example, Hilgard has presented a list of fourteen "statements" or generalizations about learning about which he thinks there would be general agreement among learning theorists.[6] Most of these statements may be seen to have ready application in the management of the school learning process. For example, No. 4, "Learning under the control of reward is usually preferable to learning under the control of punishment," constitutes a major part of the scientific basis for "programmed instruction" and the teaching machine.

2. Ernest R. Hilgard, *Theories of Learning*, 2d ed. (New York: Appleton-Century-Crofts, 1956).

3. B. F. Skinner, *The Behavior of Organisms* (New York: Appleton-Century, 1938), and *Science and Human Behavior* (New York: Macmillan Co., 1953).

4. L. L. Thurstone, *The Reliability and Validity of Tests* (Ann Arbor, Michigan: Edwards Bros., 1931).

5. Frederic M. Lord, A Theory of Test Scores, *Psychometric Monographs*, No. 7, 1952.

6. Hilgard, *Theories of Learning*, pp. 485–87.

What is still unavailable is a series of mathematically expressed statements or formulas which would systematize the relations between individual differences and learning rates under various conditions. Elsewhere I have attempted to sketch the outlines of a system which would describe the degree of learning as a function of five generalized variables: individual aptitude (stated in terms of time required to achieve criterion performance on a task under optimal learning conditions), individual general intelligence (conceived as the individual's ability to comprehend instruction), perseverance (time engaged in active learning), the quality of instruction, and opportunity (time afforded for learning).[7] Thus far, this remains merely a conceptual model. Much research would be required to confirm or modify the proposed functional relations and to supply the necessary parametric information. Nevertheless, we have available the techniques for securing this kind of information, and thus it looks as if the development of a parametric system for describing learning and individual differences is possible. Presumably that system could be refined to such an extent that it would be possible to make accurate predictions of the course of learning for given individuals under given conditions. If this could be done, educational psychology would acquire a structural coherence that would enhance its stature as a discipline.

3. *The methodology of educational psychology.*—Of the four criteria of a discipline that we are considering, the one referring to methodology is the one that is most clearly met by educational psychology. Indeed, it can be said that methods in educational psychology have proliferated while effective applications of these methods have been much less frequent. There exist extensive rationales and prescriptions for developing measuring instruments, for sampling behavior, for designing experiments, and for analyzing and summarizing data. Given the time, facilities, research talent, and necessary cooperation on the part of school authorities,

7. John B. Carroll, "A Model of School Learning," *Teachers College Record,* LXIV (1963), 723-33.

we are prepared to set up an efficient design to test nearly any hypothesis that might be reasonably proposed. Furthermore, we have the tools and techniques for implementing the program of research which I sketched out just above—the program to discover the parameters of school learning in relation to aptitude, intelligence, motivation, and other variables.

Only one caution may be noted, but it is a large caution. A heuristic method for obtaining new knowledge ought to contain a procedure for leading the researcher to ask the right questions. Educational psychology is deficient in theories which can generate useful research questions. For example, it has been pointed out by several research workers that fifty years or more of research on the problem of teacher competence have yielded very little of practical use; they suggest that this may mean that research workers have failed to ask the right questions in this area. The very promising results on teacher competence which are issuing from the work of Washburne and his collaborators at Brooklyn College [8] would on the other hand exemplify a kind of research which has been guided by detailed and well-considered theories. Theories with heuristic value in educational psychology will apparently have to be rather complex theories, appealing to several levels of interaction between variables.

It will remain true, of course, that the development of good theories requires ingenuity and not merely the ability to see gaps in a pre-existing structure.

4. *Tools and techniques for practical application.*—In respect to this criterion also, educational psychology measures up to our requirements. One can identify many kinds of tools and techniques which are sufficiently well developed and standardized to be used confidently in practical situations. The bulk of these tools are what we call *tests*—tests of ability, personality, interest, attitude, and

8. Carleton Washburne and Louis M. Heil, "What Characteristics of Teachers Affect Children's Growth?" *School Review,* LXVIII (1960), 420–28.

achievement. Tests vary widely in quality, and even the best of them could stand improvement in some respects, but the very fact that criteria exist by which we can identify the better tests is another stone in building the edifice of a discipline. The tools and techniques of educational psychology also include teaching devices, such as reading pacers, and teaching machines and techniques of programming.

One could wish, however, for a closer nexus between educational and psychological theory, on the one hand, and the tools and techniques, on the other. Tools and techniques get most closely identified with their discoverers or developers, rather than with broad principles or theories. For example, in the field of intelligence testing it should now be possible to set up standardized procedures for measuring each of a series of ability factors, named in terms of the kind of behavior or achievement involved in each case. One could then abandon the practice of associating names with particular assemblages of test materials, such as Binet, Otis, Terman, and Thurstone. In some branches of science it is quite appropriate to name certain objects or procedures after their discoverers—the fissure of Rolando, the Van Allen radiation belts, Babinski's test and so on—but in such cases the object or procedure identified is something that would not have changed its character had it been discovered by another. It is unlikely, however, that various psychological tests would have been developed in the same way had they been developed by persons other than their originators. Furthermore, psychological techniques must be constantly refined and modified to keep pace with the development of psychology. Ideally, they should be constructed according to rules independent of the predilections of any given set of investigators, deriving only from relevant psychological theory. This process of the standardization of the techniques of educational psychology *by reference to theory* would further increase the stature of educational psychology as a discipline and incidentally increase the comparability of research findings from different laboratories.

It would be easy to be iconoclastic about the view of educational psychology as a discipline which I have presented here. Perhaps educational psychology is a discipline, but a relatively empty, futile, and useless one. It has sometimes been claimed that educational psychology is nothing more than "putting what everybody knows in language which nobody can understand." [9] In a dissertation completed at Yale University in 1950, W. W. Lynch showed that freshmen in teachers colleges, even before taking any courses in educational psychology, were able to answer questions on certain parts of the content of these courses quite accurately, and at any rate as well as seniors who had taken three years of educational psychology courses.[10]

Scrutiny reveals, however, that the test questions on which freshmen did as well as seniors were the vaguest of generalizations, like the following:

(T or F)   Teaching may improve methods of reasoning.
(T or F)   Readiness for learning may be suggested by pupil interest.
(T or F)   Periodic reports to parents from the school should include only the data on children's subject matter achievement.

Those items of content where seniors showed significant achievements in knowledge over the freshmen tended to have to do with matters of special terminology, names of tests, and other technical details. Lynch even reported that in some cases seniors had a greater amount of misinformation than freshmen as a result of taking educational measurement courses; for example, 96 per cent of the freshmen accepted the proposition that "drill facilitates learning" whereas only 76 per cent of seniors recognized the "correctness" of the proposition. It is possible, of course, that Lynch was wrong in thinking this statement correct, and that the 24 per

9. Walter S. Monroe, *Teaching-Learning Theory and Teacher Education 1890–1950* (Urbana: University of Illinois Press, 1952), p. 379.
10. W. W. Lynch, Jr., "The Development of Proficiency in Educational Psychology," (Unpublished Ph.D. Dissertation, Yale University, 1950).

cent of seniors who marked it incorrect were at least correct in recognizing it as too easy a generalization.

Let us not be too hasty, however, in drawing the conclusion that educational psychology is a recitation of the obvious. Lynch's results are principally a commentary on the relatively poor quality of the test items he had to use, or perhaps on the lack of intellectual starch in the teachers college courses in educational psychology that were involved in his study. They do not necessarily imply a condemnation of all educational psychology courses or deny the possibility that educational psychology is a discipline. They should put us on notice, however, that the content of educational psychology that we present to students must be scrutinized for its informativeness, and also for its relevance to the solution of educational problems which cannot be adequately solved on the basis of so-called common sense alone.

The question that will be asked at this point is this: Does educational psychology have anything to say, anywhere in the spectrum of educational problems, that teachers dare not at their peril, so to speak, overlook? Bridge builders dare not neglect physical laws and information about the strength of physical materials. Are there similar matters which teachers ought not to neglect? It might be thought risky for a speaker to set forth such a challenge for himself. It is particularly risky when occasion provides opportunity to answer only in general terms, or with an unsatisfying set of instances.

My general answer is, Yes, there are many findings and principles in the discipline of educational psychology that teachers ought not to neglect. Facts about learning, about personality development, about types of reaction to frustration, about kinds of learned abilities, about teaching for transfer, about the construction and use of tests, and many other aspects of psychology can, I believe, be presented in sufficient richness of detail to be informative and effective in furthering better teaching. Teachers ought not to neglect these facts, but they *do*—partly because they often lack time to consider or plan their actions in the light of these principles, or because in education there are not the kinds of controls on teachers which insure that they take account of findings from educational psychology. There are few controls, for example, which insure that teachers always determine the readiness of children to receive a given level of instruction, always present new information in such a way that the student can constantly check the correctness of his learning, always give properly designed achievement tests, or always take into account the possibility that aggression is a reaction to frustration.

If we cannot insure that teachers will take adequate account of the technology of instruction which comes from the discipline of educational psychology, it is conceivable that at least some of this technology can be built into the materials and media of instruction. The research on the readability of prose has had a significant effect on the writing of textbooks, even though some would say that the effect has not been uniformly beneficial. There is much to be learned about the presentation of verbal material. Recently a thesis at Harvard by David Purpel demonstrated that the most profitable way of using time in the presentation of social studies case material at the junior high school level is *not* to repeat every statement in its original or a reworded form, but to give concrete illustrations of generalizations wherever possible. We are learning that in the teaching of many subjects—arithmetic, physics, and so on—the use of concrete models like the Cuisenaire rods or the ripple tank can make an enormous difference between good and bad teaching. The teaching machine is offered as a physical embodiment of a science of learning.

These developments point to a generalization which probably applies in every instance in which uses of basic science are sought in practical action: the basic science itself grows and is fed by the efforts to put it to practical use. Countless examples could be given of important developments in psychology which have stemmed from practical educational needs—the development of mental tests, the development of learning theory, and now the development of teaching machines. Psychology, especially educational psychology, has at least as much to learn from the practice of education as it has to teach it.

We have mentioned some of the difficulties in applying educational psychology to practical problems. In many instances, the difficulty lies in a lack of adequate research information. Most educational researchers would concede that upon such important topics as the selection and training of teachers and the evaluation of their success, the programming of instruction, and the diagnosis of children's learning difficulties, there is still a near-dearth of solid research information. Sometimes what is needed is an interpretation of research which will be intelligible to the potential user. It has often seemed to me that writers of test manuals address themselves more to their professional colleagues than to the ultimate consumer of such tests.

We also frequently meet the argument that specific educational problems are too complex, with too many interacting variables, to be soluble by the application of scientific knowledge. If this is so, it means that educational research must pay increasingly greater attention to interactions between variables. But even if knowledge becomes more precise, there will always remain cases to which no formula can be applied. Clinical psychologists do not let this fact deter them in their efforts to build and test complex hypotheses to help them in the understanding of individual cases. Meehl, of course, has demonstrated that actuarial prediction—by formula, as it were—is usually as good as, if not better than, clinical prediction.[11] But in the absence of the information which is needed to yield actuarial prediction, the judgment of the practitioner will be aided when he is steeped in the "sensitizing" concepts of educational psychology. For example, a teacher faced with the problem of how to help a minority-group child adjust and respond to what appears to be discriminatory attitudes on the part of other children, will possibly be better able to cope with this problem if he or she is

11. Paul E. Meehl, *Clinical* versus *Statistical Prediction* (Minneapolis: University of Minnesota Press, 1954).

aware of such concepts as scape-goat mechanisms, peer group status needs, and so on. Educational psychology does not inform the teacher exactly how to use these concepts in a particular case; it merely suggests that these concepts are relevant. As far as the training of teachers is concerned, there is the clear implication that not only do the concepts need to be learned as abstractions, but they also need to be illustrated in a variety of practical contexts so that teachers will be more likely to perceive their relevance to new situations. The application of scientific knowledge in actual situations by practitioners is clearly a problem of "transfer of learning"; much that can be said about transfer of learning in general can also be said about this particular situation, and when we teach educational psychology we must teach for transfer, with a vengeance.

In conducting such a complex and multi-dimensional enterprise as education, and in "applying" knowledge from other disciplines, one is never quite sure as to the source of the knowledge one is seeking to apply. Indeed, one is seldom conscious of the process of application: *application* (and likewise the word *transfer,* in transfer of training) is a word in a metalanguage of analysis, not a word corresponding to any separate event or process. Thus, if I devise a lesson in English grammar, it is difficult to identify the actual steps in which I "apply" my knowledge of educational psychology, or my knowledge of structural linguistics, or of logical analysis. Conscious attention to this kind of application would possibly inhibit me in the preparation of the lesson, but I believe I will produce a better lesson if I have a knowledge of certain aspects of educational psychology and of structural linguistics. For example, I would begin in the lesson by informing the student what he is going to learn and why it is important; I would proceed to present simple, systematic variations in the material so that the student would perceive the basis for the concept he is to form; I would attempt to elicit responses from the student which would indicate his attainment of the concept; and I would be careful to arrange that he is informed of the correctness or incorrectness of his responses.

The foregoing is, of course, a speculation. Actually, there is little or no research evidence as to the effect of educational psychology courses in promoting skill and competence in teaching lessons, and precious little research on its possible effect on skill in classroom management. No one seems to have bothered to set up appropriate experimental designs to measure these effects. The elaborate and interesting research of Ojemann and others on the effects of training teachers in a causal approach to the understanding of human behavior [12] suffered somewhat by not having adequate measures of the terminal effects, although it seemed to suggest that these effects were indeed significantly dependent upon the special training which the teachers had had. Until we have much more research testimony concerning the operational effectiveness of educational psychology in training teachers to handle practical educational problems, we shall have to be content to regard it as a discipline with a large but by no means wholly realized potential for effective application, and we shall continue to teach educational psychology to teachers with a mixture of pious optimism and subdued embarrassment.

COMMENTS *J. M. Stephens*

I take it that my job is not to remind you of the important things in Mr. Carroll's paper or to utter an enthusiastic, "How true!" Rather, I am supposed to raise points that call for elaboration or clarification, and to call attention to matters that may demand further thought. For this reason, I shall devote most of my time to the

12. R. H. Ojemann, E. E. Levitt, W. H. Lyle, and M. F. Whiteside, "The Effects of 'Causal' Teacher-Training Program and Certain Curricular Changes on Grade School Children," *Journal of Experimental Education,* XXIV (1955), 95–114.

first quarter of the paper—the part in which I see most need for clarification and the part in which Mr. Carroll has most to say about the *general* question of this conference. I realize, of course, that Mr. Carroll himself does not wish to emphasize this part of the paper. I shall spend less time on the larger part of his paper that deals with educational psychology. Here I find little to question and would be tempted merely to exhort you to heed what had been said. In looking at the roster of psychologists scheduled to appear, moreover, I feel sure that the bearings of psychology on our conference will not be neglected.

Mr. Carroll provides us with four useful criteria by which we can judge education's claims to be a discipline. But I am not always sure of the question to which Mr. Carroll applies his criteria. Most of the time, I think, he is asking, Is there disciplinary material in the field of education? Less often does he turn to the question of education as *a* discipline. I hope, by the way, that that little word *a* did not get into the title by accident. I am assuming that we are genuinely concerned about the distinctiveness or severality of the discipline of education. Can we find a recognizable entity that we can call *a* discipline of education? The problem is not unlike that of deciding whether or not a given geographical area such as Hamilton or Jersey City is *a* community. We can always find aspects of community life, but to decide upon the relative severality of a given area is a different matter.

Mr. Carroll's first criterion does deal with this problem of severality. If education is to be considered a discipline we must be able to define its sector. There must be some way of marking our area off from other areas. Obviously this severance cannot be clear-cut, and the fences established must have many gates and must permit considerable traffic in and out of the area. But the boundaries should be there.

The next criterion deals with the degree of structure to be found within the area thus marked off. And here, Mr. Carroll sees enough structure, or promise of structure, to permit education to pass the test. To use this criterion to decide about education as a discipline, however, I think we would have to know more about the kind of structures Mr. Carroll has in mind. Suppose, following the first criterion, we consider education as a bounded area. Suppose further that this area overlaps other areas, such as history, psychology, philosophy, political science, or sociology. Now where must this structure reside? The information in educational psychology, for instance, may have a structure that is an integral part of the structures within general psychology. The same may be true for each of the other intersecting areas. Would structures of this kind permit Mr. Carroll to say, "Yes. Education meets the criterion of structure"? Or would he have to find, and does he find, structures which not only lie partially within the area, but which are part and parcel of the area? Would he have to find some substantial structure which incorporates the various segments of psychology, philosophy, and so forth, which lie within the area? To permit us to speak of education as a discipline, would this latter structure have to be prominent in relation to the structures that cross the boundary of the central circle?

I ask the same questions about the third criterion, the possession of methods for gathering information and for structuring it. Is it enough to show that history and philosophy each has its own methods and that these methods are used in the history or philosophy of education? Or, if we are to say that a subject is a discipline, must we see some relation between the methods used within the larger circle? Should these relations between methods be substantial in comparison to the relations to be found within the field of history or philosophy?

I will hurry past the criterion of utility. Mr. Carroll shows that this is a frightening question to raise. I hope that it is irrelevant to the question of what is a discipline, and I wonder if it is true, as Mr. Carroll suggests, that the development of measuring instruments stems largely from a concern with utility. At any rate, this criterion seems to give little trouble with respect to the distinctiveness or severality of a discipline.

My next question deals with the sufficiency of these criteria. Can we decide about education as a discipline on the basis of these criteria alone? Offhand, I would think we would have to bring in something like patterns of communication, training, and recruitment. If a discipline suggests a field of training as well as an area of investigation, then *a* discipline would suggest a fairly well defined area of training and related forms of communication. To decide whether or not ours is *a* discipline, we should try to decide whether or not the patterns of training and communication pay any attention to our boundary. Are the communications between Kuethe and Price substantial in relation to the communication between Kuethe and Deese or between Price and Siegler? I have in mind some sort of inverted F-ratio in which the within communication should be large in relation to the between communication. Personally, I would plot the communication and training patterns first, and draw my boundary afterwards.

But I am not supposed to be telling you what Mr. Carroll should have said. Let me try to get back into line by asking him if he could decide upon the distinctiveness of a discipline without paying considerable attention to the pattern of communication.

And now I should like to turn to the special problem of educational psychology. Dr. Carroll presents educational psychology as an applied science. Surely it is that, but is it only that? Does it not also have a disinterested feature that should be considered, especially in a conference such as this? What about the distinctive phenomena of education that call for psychological study? My own pet example of such a phenomenon is the process whereby a social institution such as the school is able to engage the mechanism of learning to be found within the student. The student comes to school equipped with the mechanisms by which learning can take place. But if education is to take place, the school must reach and manipulate those mechanisms. What psychological forces are at its disposal for this task? Questions such as these represent a distinctive area of inquiry within the larger field of psychology. Such inquiries ought to be made whether or not they hold any promise of utility. What would one call such a disinterested psychological study of basic educational phenomena?

In keeping with his concept of educational psychology as an applied field, Mr. Carroll is somewhat concerned about the many areas of psychology left unapplied by current texts. This is an interesting point and one that has received too little stress in recent years. I think the writers of texts in educational psychology might well take a second look to see if they have sold psychology short in this respect. I suspect that in the past textbook writers have had in mind two criteria in selecting topics. For each prospective topic they may have asked first, What is the probability that students are already familiar with this topic? Second, What is the probability that the topic will prove useful? This would lead to a concentration on the topics in the upper left corner and the neglect of many that had high applicability but were considered to be already familiar.

Turning to an incidental point, I suspect Mr. Carroll has overstressed the overlapping of educational psychology and the basic study of learning. Thorndike's tremendous impact in both fields might suggest such an overlapping. But I wonder if there would be much general correlation between prominence in the field of learning and interest in educational applications.

It is a brave educational psychologist who raises the question of the utility of his subject. And Mr. Carroll's treatment of this topic is clearly courageous. It is also honest and sobering. I share his subdued embarrassment and his feeling of relying on pious optimism. I only wonder if he has not found too much solace in listing the things that teachers should know about but probably neglect. I feel sure we could improve their verbal comprehension of these topics, and this I admit is a worthy end in itself. But I fear a behavioral test. In the hurly-burly of teaching, would our more sophisticated teachers greatly excel those who had to rely almost entirely on more primitive and pervasive guides? Teaching of one kind or another is an ancient art. Some modest competence in that art, moreover, has probably been a requirement for group survival during several thousand years. It would be surprising if the machinery necessary for this basic teaching is something that must all be acquired as optional extra equipment. Much of this necessary machinery probably comes firmly built into the standard factory product.

VI

Education as a Discipline
Some Historical Notes

BERNARD BAILYN

THE QUESTION posed by this conference—whether or to what extent the study of education is a discipline in itself—is of peculiar importance to the historian. It leads him directly into a large and important area of investigation in his own field, for habit of mind —professional reflex, perhaps—suggests to him that the question itself has an historical dimension, that it had an origin in time and place and a development through the pressures of circumstance. When he follows this thought he discovers not merely a useful background for consideration of the question at hand, but a vital chapter in American cultural history that is little known and well worth examining for its own sake.

The origins of the present concern with education as a separate body of knowledge and methods lie in the activities of a remarkable group of men, the founders and early evangelists of professionalism in American education. These men—Ellwood Cubberley, Paul Monroe, Henry Suzzallo, W. H. Kilpatrick, to name the most prominent—whose most creative years were the first two decades of the twentieth century, had an extraordinary influence on the development of modern American culture; and they are in themselves interesting. Their external characteristics gave little indication of the energy and vision they possessed. They were men of great accomplishment, but they were moderate and measured in manner: controlled, methodical, and rather humorless. They had glimpsed the promised land, and they pursued it with passion. Embodiments of the Protestant ethic, they became fantastically successful academic entrepreneurs. By World War I they were the captains of a vast educational industry.

What shaped their purpose and intensified their energy was a belief and a vision which became in the end a great administrative enterprise. At the root of their thought was the conviction that the study of education was not merely, in our more narrowly academic phrase, a discipline, but something grander than that, more esoteric and more important. Education, they claimed, was, properly, nothing less than a *science,* and its methods should be scientific. This was the dominant theme of a number of influential books and of many articles published at the turn of the century in such new and (strange as it may now seem) exciting periodicals as Nicholas Murray Butler's *Educational Review,* G. Stanley Hall's *Pedagogical Seminary,* and the University of Chicago's *School Review.* In these writings there is a consistent pattern of discussion. There is, first, a description of the traditional low esteem of education, a subject so long seen, as one writer put it, as a "drudge at the academic hearth . . . whose highest recognition in the great universities has usually been as the handmaid of philosophy"; second, an explanation of this situation in the subject's lack of "a solid body of scientific knowledge and universally accepted principles"; then some demonstration of possibilities and progress ("during the past ten years the opportunities for truly scientific work in education have been shown as never before, methods have been demonstrated, and in part the foundations of a science have been laid"); and finally, somewhere—in the introduction or conclusion—an exhortation to the effect that "with the nucleus of solid scientific contributions that now exists, no university can long afford to omit courses in education from its curriculum, whether they have any practical value or not." [1]

"Science" is the key to their thought. But what was science?

1. William H. Burnham, "Education as a University Subject," *Educational Review,* XXVI (1903), 238, 241.

What did it mean in the study of education? The word was used in a great variety of ways. Sometimes it meant quite strictly induction as the basis for establishing laws of human development; sometimes it meant only a preference for facts over opinions; sometimes it meant a recognition of the central place of education in the process of evolution. The confusion in meaning could at times be painful. There was not one but "three great scientific methods" in the study of education, Paul Monroe wrote in 1910; the first was "symbolical or logical"; the second was "experimental"; and the third, the most recent and least developed, was "comparative"; it included, he explained, "the field of historical and sociological phenomena." [2] There was no end to the "scientific" underpinnings that could be found for the study of education. Ellwood Cubberley, the famous dean of Stanford's School of Education, made the course on "bionomics" offered by the university's president, the biologist and race theorist David Starr Jordan, a flat requirement for all students of education. And Cubberley saw his own academic work in education as correlative to the subjects he had first taught in college: physiology, physics, chemistry, and geology.[3]

Despite the confusion in terminology, these evangelists of professionalism in education did have considerable evidence that something new and academically respectable was happening in the world of pedagogy. There were signs on all sides that the study of education was entering a new and elevated stage of development. G. Stanley Hall, reporting in 1901 on the "collection, diffusion, and increase of the scientific knowledge of childhood" for which he and his colleagues had been responsible, stated without exaggeration that "during the last twenty years between two and three hundred investigations represented by as many books and published memoirs have emanated from Clark University." [4] But Hall represented only one school, one group of theories and experiments. In

2. Paul Monroe, "Opportunity and Need for Research Work in the History of Education," *Pedagogical Seminary,* XVII (1910), 55.
3. Jesse B. Sears and Adin D. Henderson, *Cubberley of Stanford* (Stanford: Stanford University Press, 1957), pp. 15, 22 ff., Chaps. V–VII.
4. G. Stanley Hall, "General Outline of the New Child Study Work of Clark University," *Pedagogical Seminary,* XVII (1910), 160.

the same field, psychology, there were also, of course, William James and the even more "scientific" E. L. Thorndike. And there were Dewey in philosophy, Ward and Small in sociology, and in history the group around Paul Monroe at Teacher's College eager to apply to education the rigorous techniques of the master historical scientists at the Johns Hopkins University.

Fortified by this evidence of "scientific" endeavor applicable, if not already applied, to the field of education, these educators sought for their subject the full apparatus of an autonomous academic discipline. Nationwide and regional professional organizations necessary for setting standards and disseminating specialized information were becoming standard equipment for the traditional academic groups: why not for education? They were quickly created or expanded from rudimentary beginnings. Professional journals were obviously necessary; by the first World War there were several with national circulation and many with more restricted audiences. Above all there was the need for proper institutional arrangements by which to train the new professionals—arrangements that would reflect the new respectability and autonomy of the study of education within the academic world. Such institutions appeared almost overnight. Normal schools, in the mid-nineteenth century often indistinguishable from ungraded common schools, acquired new standards, new content, and new ambitions. First they became, in effect, junior colleges; and then, by the workings of some wonderful counter-Greshamism, tended to disappear altogether into teachers colleges qualified to grant the bachelor's degree or into departments and faculties of education in the existing colleges and universities. By 1920 there were forty-six teachers colleges; and all but the most amoebic liberal arts colleges and universities had divisions of education complete with full professorial chairs—regular thrones in such powerful institutions as Teachers College, and the Faculty of Education at the University of Chicago —and decanal jurisdictions.

The result was remarkable. The study of education leapt ahead on all fronts, stimulated and supported by the intellectual and institutional force built up by this first generation of professional educators. Great good resulted: a broadening and deepening of the knowledge of educational processes and rapid improvement in the practice of teaching as new information and expert analyses of experience were disseminated through an increasingly well-trained, unified, and self-conscious profession.

But then, in the passage of time, limits were found and a reaction set in. By the end of the 1920's and in the 1930's the primary assumption of the founders of professionalism in education that the study of education rests, or should rest, upon the solid intellectual basis of a science or at least a discipline of its own, came into question. The various strands of traditional scholarship that had been brought into combination in the centers of educational research either remained stubbornly separate, tied individually to their original bases, or, when removed from these roots and woven into a distinct scholarly entity called education, lost their resiliency and strength. Indeed, it seemed to many that when education took the scholarship of its origins with it into seclusion and nurtured it in isolation, a retrogression, relative to the advances in the contributing disciplines—some kind of intellectual calcification—took place. What had once been exhilarating and liberating in Dewey's thought appeared to become dogma that meant something different from what had been intended in the original scripture. What had begun as the attractive possibility of classifying the phases of personality development the better to gauge the stages of instruction, seemed to end in imprisonment by test scores. What had been undertaken as an effort to find in history the whole "conscious evolution of mankind through the educative process toward spiritual and moral ends," and hence was necessarily expected to explore the "vital connection [of education] with political, social, and industrial movements," ended in a foreshortened chronicle of pedagogical institutions so caught up in anachronisms as to make explanation impossible.[5] And, more generally, what had begun as

5. William H. Burnham and Henry Suzzallo, *The History of Education as a Professional Subject* (N.Y.: Teachers College, Columbia University, 1908), pp. 52–53, 5. Cf. Bernard Bailyn, *Education in the Forming of American Society* (Chapel Hill: University of North Carolina Press, 1960), pp. 5 ff.

an effort to achieve academic respectability and intellectual maturity through institutional autonomy, appeared to end in isolation that reduced contacts between the traditional disciplines and education, damming up the currents of intellectual life to the detriment of all.

The result, by the end of World War II, was an extreme disillusion on the part of scholars with the aims and practices of professional educators and a feeling, widely shared by the public at large, that what was needed was a total reversal, a return to the very assumption the founders of educational professionalism had so vehemently rejected, the assumption that—as it was put derisively in a classic nineteenth-century statement—"there is [no] science about [teaching] except that of the branch of learning to be taught." [6] Efforts to reverse the direction of the founders' impetus took place rapidly within the colleges and universities and in the various professional organizations of the academic community.

In recent years notable efforts have been made to break the tradition of institutional isolation by means of joint appointments between education and arts and science faculties and departments and by the creation of interfaculty or interdepartmental committees and even degree programs. Such changes have not been undertaken merely for administrative convenience; they are responses to strong intellectual currents flowing from the regular academic fields towards what has appeared to many, after years of relative isolation and neglect, the potentially rich but underdeveloped soil of education. In psychology, for example, which from the beginning has kept the closest ties with education, a recent book urging that the findings of current research be applied to the everyday problems of education has called forth a nationwide response. An entire section of the national convention of the American Sociological Association is devoting itself to the problems of education. And

6. Theodore Edson, "On the Comparative Merits of Private and Public Schools," *The Introductory Discourse and the Lectures Delivered before the American Institute of Instruction . . . 1837 . . .* (Boston, 1838), p. 95.

recently a group of professional historians, no one of whom identifies himself primarily as an historian of education, have organized themselves under foundation sponsorship as a committee to advance research and teaching in the role of education in American history. Finally, there are efforts such as the one we are presently engaged in, to gather representatives of various fields to consider the situation as a whole and to rethink the meaning of education as a discipline.

But the full implications of this great pendulum swing, this motion first towards and then away from the study of education as a separate scholarly enterprise resting on the sense of a special body of knowledge and special methods of investigation—the full implications cannot be grasped in these general terms. One must reach into the substance of the fields involved in order to see the implications with any degree of completeness. Unfortunately, I am competent to discuss the development in detail only in one field, history; but what has happened there—and what is happening now—is suggestive, I believe, of more general conclusions.

In history, one cannot avoid concluding that a process of desiccation set in as the result of the emphasis upon the peculiar concerns of education, reinforced by institutional barriers that served for two generations to limit contacts between the general practitioners of history and the specialists in education. So far has this process gone that the consequences are now perversely attractive. The general historian finds the ruling formulations of the history of education so parochial, so restricted by the presumption of special purpose, and consequently so far behind the frontiers of contemporary scholarship in the field at large that the entire subject appears to be one great and intriguing question mark. It is not merely a matter of factual accumulation and narrative coherence. It is a matter of understanding as well, so that wherever one touches the subject—even where the monographic masonry appears to be most solid—it proves to be weak and insubstantial. Everything, it seems, is out of focus, askew. Exciting possibilities open up to anyone who brings to bear on the history of education the ideas and information currently influencing the general interpretation of American history. The most important example is perhaps also the most dramatic.

The central theme, the organizing idea, of the history of American education that resulted from the work of Cubberley and his successors had at least the virtue of clarity. These writers, deeply involved in the contemporary problems of education and convinced that history contained a special message bearing on these problems, knew well what the outcome of history had been, and they sought in the past the early evidences of that conclusion. They found what they were looking for, and so wrote the story not of the emergence of the new from the old, the familiar from the unfamiliar, but of the struggle between two essentially unchanging elements, the one destined to fail, the other to triumph. What triumphed, what had to triumph, was the concept and practice of public education as they knew it: the victory, that is, of free, publicly supported and publicly controlled institutions organized into state systems and containing three distinct levels of instruction, elementary, secondary, and collegiate. It was a long battle between the forward-looking, right, and necessary on the one hand and unthinking traditionalism compounded with selfishness and bigotry on the other. The climax and victory had come in the great reform movement of the 1830's and 1840's led by Horace Mann, Henry Barnard, Calvin Wiley, and the others of that famous group.

But when one tests this formulation, approaching the story not from the point of view of the future but of the past—not from the standpoint of contemporary education, of what the historian knows happened in education, but of what the participants expected would happen—and when one places the evidence in a broad historical context, some rather disconcerting facts emerge.

The main difficulty is that gradually as one reviews that period one comes to see not so much that the facts are wrong but that the presumptions of thought are anachronistic. The meaning of key words is not that of contemporaries. The concept of "public" as we understand it did not exist before the time of Mann; it was a consequence, a creation, of the social and political struggles of Mann's time. An older, different meaning of the word was current until the middle of the nineteenth century and it persisted, side by side with the new, through at least another generation.

The word "public" in the eighteenth century had nothing necessarily to do with things that were free (that is, free of special costs), tax supported, or government controlled. It was used, in general, to indicate anything that benefitted the community as a whole, and in reference to educational institutions, only to designate the lack of legal barriers to entrance. Anyone could enter a public school (as opposed, for example, to a school restricted to the sons of the members of a guild)—anyone, that is, willing to pay whatever special fees might be required. True, there were schools in eighteenth-century America, though largely in New England, supported by taxes and managed by elected officers of government. But this was seen not as a particular kind of education but as one among a number of expedient forms that had arisen in response to peculiar economic circumstances and to an original religious concern that demanded not systems of public schools but teaching, however instituted, by which to preserve Christian civilization in the face of a threatening environment.

There was no sharp line between public and private. The two, as we would distinguish them, merged continuously. Private donations frequently supported institutions governed by public officials, and, even more commonly, the state contributed to the support of all those institutions, privately founded, owned, and managed, that it felt served to advance the general welfare, retaining only occasional visitorial powers. Indeed, it is anachronistic even to say that private and public functions overlapped and merged before the nineteenth century: the distinctions by which to make such a statement were absent. Contemporaries were aware only of a natural continuum, a subtly colored spectrum at whose barely visible extremities alone could be found what we think of as the two necessary distinctions.

What took place in the history of education in the nineteenth century was that in the course of a half-successful struggle to place education fully under government ownership, support, and management, the word "public," as applied to education, took on a new and more restricted meaning. But it was not simply the word. The concept behind it changed. It was then that the idea of public education as we know it emerged—was created. There was nothing obvious, necessary, or inevitable about this development. A feasible alternative existed. Indeed, both logic and recent history lay solidly on the side of the opponents of change. The central historical problem is not to trace the stages of the preordained ascent of a stable conception and institutional arrangement but to explain the halting, confused, and controverted demise and supersession of the existing ones.

The essential characteristics of American education before the reform movement of Mann's era are best seen at the levels of what we call secondary and higher education. There, neither public nor private education, as we think of these, was characteristic. What there was of public education was largely a matter of inert legislative or constitutional provisions written in the flush of Revolutionary enthusiasm. These enactments, requiring or permitting universities or other "literary institutions" to be founded, supported, and managed by the state, had by 1800 come to little. The active tendencies, the vital social forces, were moving in a different direction.

There was taking place during the same years, first, a remarkable multiplication of collegiate institutions—a veritable epidemic of new foundations of higher education, quantitatively probably greater than any other such movement in history—created, managed, and usually but not always supported by private, mainly denominational, groups. They appeared everywhere—in the most unlikely places: in raw, scarcely settled midwestern hamlets, in southern villages, in half-cleared mountain tracts as well as in the cities—and in numbers beyond the ability of modern scholarship to reconstruct. We can enumerate with certainty only those officially chartered by the states; of these, record has been found of 516 before 1860.

More important, because even more widespread and far less expected (indeed, for this there was no precedent at all), was the sudden appearance, the explosive proliferation, of privately sponsored and directed but often publicly supported educational institutions below the collegiate level. The historical importance of this extraordinary development in American education would be difficult to exaggerate; yet it has been almost entirely lost. In histories of education it appears only in the guise of something called "the academy movement," which is presented as a transitional phase in the history of secondary education created by "a new and prosperous middle class mercantile group" and fitting neatly between the doomed "aristocratic" Latin grammar schools of the colonial period and the emerging "democratic" high schools of modern America. But in reality this development seems to have been a powerful folk movement in which large numbers of people, organizing locally, built for themselves, without prescriptive traditions, plans, or principles of education, institutions to serve vague, unformed cultural needs.

So deeply rooted, so spontaneous, so uncontrolled and unsystematic was the movement that the resulting institutions defy clear enumeration or categorization. Henry Barnard's figures for 1850 are as good as any: he listed over 800 academies in New York, over 500 in Pennsylvania, over 400 in Massachusetts, over 300 each in Kentucky and Virginia, and over 200 each in Connecticut, Georgia, Maryland, Missouri, New Jersey, North Carolina, Ohio, South Carolina, and Tennessee. His total of 6,085 academies, served by 12,260 teachers, and enrolling over a quarter of a million students in the thirty-six states and territories is probably an understatement.

The difficulty in establishing these basic figures reflects the protean character of the institutions. Nomenclature alone is confusing, and instructional content is bewildering. The most common name was "academy," but there were also institutions in no way different from those called academies that were known as seminaries, collegiate institutions, free schools (which charged tuition), classical institutes, Franklin institutes, or just institutes. What was the level of instruction? There is no single answer; instruction was at all levels and at any level. Most can perhaps fairly be called secondary schools, but some were no better than common schools while others were, in effect, colleges. They taught, it seems, everything. The few tabulations we have of the subjects formally offered are staggering: no less than 230 subjects were taught in the Indiana academies: everything from aesthetics to zoology, including besides all standard offerings such advanced subjects as banking, metallurgy, sociology, and archaeology, and such curiosities as conchology, dialling, filigree, intellectual philosophy, pyrography, synonyms, and tissue flowers. The central point comes out most clearly perhaps from the advertisement of a Fayetteville, North Carolina, academy which promised to teach a large array of subjects "together with such other branches of education as parents may desire"—in effect, anything.[7] Most were small (the average academy in nineteenth-century Indiana had 67 students and 4.7 teachers), but many were quite large; most were coeducational, but some were not; many were boarding schools, some were not. Everything about them was various and changing. There were no regular teaching staffs: 70 per cent of the teachers, according to one calculation, left before the end of two years. Indeed, the institutions themselves were impermanent: in New York, where they were more stable than in most places, the great majority lasted between five and ten years; yet some have remained to this day.

But however strange and protean, however transient and uneven in quality these schools may have been, they were the direct,

7. Charles L. Coon, *North Carolina Schools and Academies 1790–1840: A Documentary History* (Raleigh, N.C.: Edwards and Broughton, 1915), p. 66.

natural, spontaneous and unique expression of the American people in matters of education during the first two post-Revolutionary generations. Surveying the American scene in, say, 1820, one would have had little reason to expect a different form to arise— especially one that would have a special and superior claim to being called "public." For these academies—private institutions according to our present terminology: that is, initiated by private effort and private funds, owned and managed by private individuals or boards of trustees—were understood to be and were often officially designated public, and efforts were made, with notable success in some places, to organize them into systems and to sustain them with public funds. The New York legislature in 1784 and 1787 included private academies within its plan for a state-wide educational system, instructing the regents of the state university to set up minimal qualifying rules for schools receiving state aid. In the same years Georgia, similarly, ordered what was in effect its state board of education—a body which, under the first state constitution, went under the name of the "Senatus Academicus"— to facilitate state grants to all applicant institutions. Louisiana took similar steps. And Massachusetts, which continued to subsidize Harvard, Amherst, and Williams colleges until the middle of the nineteenth century, in 1797 arranged to give every private academy that met certain stated requirements one-half a township of public land as an endowment.

Such arrangements and the assumptions behind them persisted even after modern forms of public schooling had been introduced and were in process of adoption. In 1859 an official interpretation of the original status of the Massachusetts academies correctly stated that they were "regarded as in many respects, and to a considerable extent, public schools; as a part of an organized system of public and universal education; as opening the way for all the people to a higher order of instruction than the common schools can supply and as a complement to them . . . ." As late as 1874 the New York Regents were arguing that incorporated academies "may . . . be regarded as public institutions to all intents and purposes for which they are established." And to this day, the same view persists in Maine and is an important source of controversy.[8]

Independent, for the most part denominational, colleges and the great congeries of private-public institutions known as academies were the almost universal forms of American education above the elementary level before the Civil War. To describe and analyze them not as a background for the more permanent institutions that were to follow—not as links between other things— but as social institutions of first importance in themselves, institutions which shaped the development of American culture and without which one cannot understand the rest—to analyze the early nineteenth-century colleges and academies in this way is a difficult but rewarding task that lies ahead for the historian. At the present time so little of the complete history of these institutions is known that one can hardly suggest even the outline of the story as it will eventually emerge. But this much, at least, is clear. The guidelines for the historian probing these problems of American education lie outside the area of education itself; the story as a whole lies deeply and broadly embedded in the cultural soil of nineteenth-century America, and it will not be grasped by one who approaches it with the special purposes of education exclusively, or even primarily, in mind.

These remarks have taken me rather far afield from the original considerations of this paper. I have gone this far in order to illustrate in my own field of history the consequences of the assumptions of the founders of professionalism in education that the study of education is, if not a science, at least a discipline in itself. For the historian, the evidence indicates that it is not; or better, that the assumption that it is, is fruitless and frustrating. He sees in the

8. Charles Hammond, *New England Academies and Classical Schools,* Fortieth Annual Report of the [Massachusetts] Board of Education . . . 1877 (Boston: Wright and Potter, 1877), p. 209; *Eighty-seventh Annual Report of the [New York] Regents of the University . . . 1874* (Albany, 1874), p. xiv.

historiography of education some stultifying consequences of such an assumption.

The study of education for the historian is not a science and it is not a discipline. Perhaps it may be described most usefully as a crossroads where the separate paths of scholarship and of the practical affairs of the society meet, to which scholars may freely move, bringing to the great work of education the knowledge and skills acquired in their own proper disciplines, and from which they may return with new insights and new questions.

COMMENTS *Wilson Smith*

It is for me indeed a pleasure to appear on this program with Professor Bailyn. Among American historians he recently has done more than anyone else to awaken interest in what we may term the "new history" of American education. In his book *Education in the Forming of American Society,* he has applied on a larger scale in our colonial period much the same kind of institutional measurement that he briefly has delineated for you this afternoon in his illustrations of the nineteenth-century academies in Indiana and in the implications for education of legal incorporation. To the historian he presents the role of education in the American past in a way that is free from cant and jargon. His little book has already proved to be a fresh breeze to those who have long been dissatisfied with the low state of educational history. It is an exciting prospect that he opens to historians who are coming to this area of interest from social and intellectual history. I admire Mr. Bailyn's use of the materials of educational history so much that I venture the prediction that his approach to this subject will be *the* approach of academic historians for the next decade. What he has done is to rescue the tired, almost lifeless, figure of the history of education from the waters of professional self-

centeredness and doctrinaire presentation. He has brought this figure to the shoreline of historiographical respectability. And he has
revived it with a sense of the fullness of history and with the excitement of a newly liberated outlook.

In commenting on his paper I should like to begin where Mr.
Bailyn leaves off. I hope that in so doing these remarks will pertain
to the problems of this conference: Does the study of the history
of education, as Mr. Bailyn describes it, result in a discipline?
and, What are the relations between the study of educational history and the humanities or the social sciences?

Let me turn again to the figure of American educational history
that Mr. Bailyn has magnificently rescued and revived. As it stands,
revitalized as a new history of education, what direction in academic affairs shall it take? I trust that neither Mr. Bailyn nor I
would wish for it anything but a hearty and long existence *as*
history, aware of its own complexity, its breadth of interest, and
its opportunity to explain the ways in which men have chosen to
transmit their culture to succeeding generations.

If under our present academic conditions of entrenched special-
izations, this revived figure of educational history were sure to become strong and useful on its own, I should not worry about it. And
I would then endorse the sentiments in the last paragraph of Mr.
Bailyn's paper unreservedly. Seen only as a corpus of past event
and idea, the history of education, I agree, is not a specific branch
of instruction or one of the traditional departments of knowledge.
And it is not even a field. If it is none of these things, however, I am
worried about its future. My concern arises not because it is home-
less in academic life; rather my worry stems from one inescapable
fact about history. It is that as surely as men *make* history, it is men
who tell and *write* history.

Mr. Bailyn, I think, would join me in the hope that those who
will write and have the custody of the history of education will be
historians with training in the liberal arts or in graduate departments of history. At least at present they are the ones who would

seem to offer the best experience for producing the new history of education that is seen through Mr. Bailyn's paper.

But even if we were somehow assured that a liberal education would be part of the equipment of everyone who would write the new history of education, I would still be worried. I would want to have some reason to believe, even if no assurance, that liberally educated historians would continue to pursue educational history in the effective way that Mr. Bailyn has begun. In seeking evidence for this encouragement I would look to the history of academic historians in this country to find what their professional past tells us about the likelihood of their nurturing the new history of education. Here briefly is what I might find.

First of all, we know that the attachment to narrow purposes and guild aims on the part of the founders of professionalism in American education, of which Mr. Bailyn speaks, had its counterpart around the turn of this century in the regional pride or the narrow nationalism sometimes bordering on jingoism among some general American historians. We must remember, further, that when exaggerated claims for the history of educational institutions came from our educational entrepreneurs around 1900, such claims were the result, in one sense, of an urge that has beset many a profession in its infancy, including the profession of history. This is the urge to establish one's own standards, group interests, and to make one's professional status secure. It may be well to recall also that until only recently general American historians were peculiarly wedded to one-dimensional political accounts of our past, based chiefly upon the institution of the presidency, in much the same way that educational historians were focusing narrowly upon the history of the curriculum or of school administration.

The professional past of the educational entrepreneur and that of the academic historian can be compared in another brief way that may serve us here. The attachment to science on the part of these "early evangelists of professionalism in American education," as Mr. Bailyn calls them, also had its counterpart among American historians of their day. We need only to remind ourselves of the detailed forecasts for mankind plotted by Henry Adams on the basis of physical laws, or of the claims for the aesthetic superiority of technological civilizations made by other historians in the years when our great industrial empires and fortunes were being made. Then, a bit later, the extremes in the writing of history to which determinisms of the economic variety were pushed by lesser known historians than Charles Beard, to whom "economic determinism" is insistently and wrongly imputed, were as misleading for academic history as was the so-called science of the captains of educational industry.

My point in this, of course, is not that two wrongs make a right. It is simply that sometimes fads and fashions in American historiography have been as strong as fads and fashions in administering the schools or in writing the history of education.

What conclusions do I draw from this? They are, first, that the new history of education will be only as perceptive and as candid as the men who write it. Second, I conclude that since there have been historiographical shortcomings among *all* historians, not just among educational historians, the chances are that *some* historians of the new history of education, no matter what their academic preparation, will come a cropper, to the detriment of this new history. Third, I think that since we always have to risk the bad writing of history as well as the good—because all of this fortunately goes on under the sanction of academic freedom—we can perhaps try to erect a safeguard or two to try to protect the history of education from repeating the errors of its own past.

One of the safest guards against the bad writing of educational history that I can think of in our present circumstances—and I stress present circumstances in the United States—is to treat the history of education as a new discipline. Here of course is where Mr. Bailyn and I seem to part company. He has held that treating the history of education as a narrow discipline and as a science led to its undoing. I agree with his historical reasons for saying this. Yet I hold that we now must treat this subject at least as a field of study, if not as a new academic discipline.[9]

Why so? The main reason, I think, is simply that times have changed. Times may once have invited an overly-specialized view of their field to the founders of educational history as a separate study in this country. Times demand the opposite now. Men who now are writing history, with a few great exceptions, tend to become extremely specialized in their interests. This was not quite as true of the historical guild, although it was becoming so, at the turn of this century. Nowadays, it seems to me, since happily men still, not machines, write history, we do well to give the liberally trained historian as broad a reference point, as wide a range of sources, and as imaginative a view of history as possible. And for what better subject than the new history of education can the historian make use of them? Why not make the historian of education akin to the general practitioner, or general diagnostician, in medicine whose decline is so frequently regretted by many patients of medical specialists? Such a generalist, to employ a Madison Avenue term, would, I suggest, not find the history of education, conceived as a discipline, "fruitless and frustrating." I think he might find it fruitful and liberating. For, as Mr. Bailyn points out in the conclusion of his paper, the historical study of education is a crossroads. To my mind it lies where the roads of humane learning and practical affairs cross. That with its central location it should invite the search for a coherent body of historical knowledge, is to me as natural and necessary as that history itself should be considered a coherent subject of study or an academic discipline. Perhaps coherence in the historical study of education may not be attained, but the *search* for coherence enables me to view the study as a discipline. I think that whatever risks we take of inviting the old cant and narrowness of view to return to educational history by treating it as if it were a discipline are far out-

9. I am using discipline only in the loose, administrative sense, as a branch of instruction or department of knowledge.

weighed by the potential advantages of study in this field. I think this because the subject itself is so broadly involved with so many aspects or the humanities and the social sciences. It is even conceivable to me that one day an autonomous and broad academic department of discipline in the history of education could be established in a university that would be at least as legitimate as any one of the new fields (and here I admit that opinions vary) of American studies, or humanistic studies, or Far Eastern studies.

It remains only for me to suggest that whereas the historical study of education fifty years ago was conceived as a narrow discipline and consequently brought out the worst in its followers, today the same study, broadly conceived in the new way depicted by Mr. Bailyn, can bring out the best in them. I mean by this that since the new history of education is a crossroads subject to which representatives of the humanities and the social sciences can bring their talents and insights, the very breadth of learning and of interest that it encompasses can make the new historian of education a valuable commodity in today's intellectual marketplace. For not only must he be a good historian, he also may come to see himself as a representative of humane learning in our technical and specialized society. When this happens he will be wedded to the life of the intellect and respectful of it in the past. It will unfailingly excite him. It will put him in the company of other historians, indeed of all academic men who have this commitment and this excitement about their lives, a commitment and an excitement that his vocationally-directed predecessors in the history of education did not fully share.

Such an ideal scholar, were he present now, would, I am sure, join me in paying tribute to the truly pioneering work of Mr. Bailyn for the new history of education. And I think that such a scholar might say, deftly and clearly, that when subject matter is presented as coherently and discussed as cogently as Mr. Bailyn did this afternoon, it surely deserves to be treated as a field of study or as a discipline.

PART THREE

Education as Academic Discipline or Profession

VII

Is Education a Discipline?[1]

EVERETT C. HUGHES

Is EDUCATION a discipline? What are the relations between other fields of study and the study of education?

These two questions have been put to us. My first impulse was to dispose of the first with a flat "No" followed by a sentence or two of argument, before proceeding to consideration of the relations of certain kinds of social study to the study of education. I did not follow that impulse; the question becomes more and more important as one gives it thought.

The argument would have been—indeed, it is—that education is one of the major human arts, or complex of arts, but not a discipline. In part, education is custodial care of the young. This is an activity that is increasingly delegated to people other than parents and for a longer period of the child's life than ever before. The school-leaving age is continually being raised, so that nearly all teen-agers are in the custody of public institutions for a good many hours a day. American colleges and universities accept, all too willingly and aggressively, personal custody of young people in their twenties, decreeing the hours of their comings and goings, the objects for which they may organize, and the thoughts which they may think (or at least, express). A young person may escape a

1. I have worked so closely with Howard S. Becker and Blanche Geer that I cannot with certainty say whether an idea came from one or the other of them, or whether it just grew out of our common talk.

good deal of this custody by marrying while he is still going to school or college; the dean of men will then lose interest in the hours he keeps, but they will still count him in and out of the classroom, and his teachers will assign him little daily chores of reading and chide him for not doing them. Such close supervision of college and university students appears amazing to visitors from abroad, as amazing as the freedom which we allow our young children.

The other great art in this complex is the imparting of knowledge, skills, and sentiments. Perhaps there are better ways to word it—the creation of opportunities for learning might be one. This activity is also expanding. There is much more knowledge of certain kinds to be imparted, and we are trying to impart it to a greater proportion of the population than ever before. Because of the rate of technological change, subjects do not stay learned. An increasing number of people are busy learning new things even about the work which they once knew well; they are running the race against obsolescence. Not fewest among these late-learners, or re-learners, are the great numbers of women who, after a spell of child-bearing and rearing, return to work, older and wiser and very industrious, but without seniority and obsolete by a decade. At any rate, the number of people engaged in professional teaching is greatly expanded, as are the subjects they teach and the kinds of people to whom they teach them. Along with this increase, has come a great self-consciousness about methods of teaching and a great deal of experimenting with new techniques, including the use of electronic communication and teaching machines.

The struggle to control the sentiments of the rising generation is likewise engaged in perhaps more self-consciously and on a greater scale than ever before. There are people who make great claims of success in this activity, and who devote a good deal of money to research on it.

Education is, indeed, a major complex of arts. Like the other great arts, it is not a discipline in the sense of offering a single order of phenomena which, when observed and/or manipulated in a systematic way, yield a body of consistent theory. In this respect, education is like the other great practical arts—looking after the sick, keeping order, and distributing justice. All of them, however, give rise to a variety of disciplines and, in turn, use many of their results. These arts are the very springs of human curiosity; they are also great consumers of man's best intellectual and scientific efforts. None of these arts, moreover, is ever completely under the control of the human will, the will of one man or of some small group of men, or even of society at large through its instruments. Yet control over these arts is sought in all societies. The manner of practicing them is the very stuff of the clash of wills and interests; thus, the stuff of politics. Any of these arts is bigger and more perennial than any of the special disciplines.

For disciplines, while they may be established as going concerns within universities, and while each may seek to prove that it was in the beginning, is now, and ever shall be, are passing things. New ones sprout; old ones merge into one another. It is common talk in the physical and biological sciences that the interesting work is being done on the raw edges between the traditional (although still young) disciplines. This is not interdisciplinary work, but work on new frontiers by men who associate with each other because of their interest in the problems at hand; "interdisciplinary work" implies that each party to it means to respect the other's boundaries, while seeing to it that his own discipline gets its share of money, attention, and space in publications. Interdisciplinary work generally means that the parties are determined not to merge their disciplines. If disciplines do not merge, it means either that no intellectual progress is being made, or that there is resistance to reorganization of the university and of research bodies in a way to correspond to the present and emerging state of the frontiers of knowledge. I mean to suggest that organization of the university by disciplines should itself be a matter of study, something on which we keep an open mind. It can choke progress of both the disciplines and the great arts.

Who knows what the disciplines of social science of the future will be? Or the divisions of the sciences of life or of the physical world? Who even knows whether life, society, and the physical world will always be studied so separately as now? Yet we can be quite certain that humans, if there are any, will gather into societies which will have need of the great fundamental arts of which one is education. In any kind of society likely to exist in the future, there will be self-conscious concern over the processes by which people learn and over the ways of organizing the institutions of custody and learning. Education is more enduring than any discipline. To try to cram education into the shell of any discipline is to put the grander into the lesser, the eternal into the temporary.

One might be astonished that the people who are concerned with education should want to bring themselves down in the world by asking that their work be recognized as among the disciplines. Yet it is not surprising, for we are in a period in which professions stand high and in which many occupations, old and new, seek professional standing. As an occupation strives for professional standing, it generally seeks, and may get, a place in the institutions called universities. It will usually claim that the work of the profession rests upon a discipline, perhaps upon a science. Indeed, the rising new professions have brought many aspects of social life under scientific scrutiny; without the pressure of new professions for recognition among the academic disciplines, our universities might be very much more narrow than they are and very much less alive to the possibilities of exploring human behavior. Teachers, the people who administer teaching, and the people who teach teachers and who study schools, have joined the merry chase to be recognized professionally and academically, the latter through declaring education a discipline. Not that many people in education do consider it a single discipline; they are more inclined, I think, to insist upon their *professional* standing. In that, they are like the people in various disciplines, notably psychology, who are now emphasizing, not their character as disciplines, but their proper place as professions. The relation of the academic disciplines to the professions is one of the fundamental problems of our time; it can be stated also as the relation of science to practice, or as the relation of basic to applied research. And this is, in part, the second question to which this paper is directed.

To that second question, I now turn, although it is not really a turning, but a continuing of the same line.

The people engaged in education, in the special sense of teaching teachers and of studying what goes on in schools, are very numerous. They have been so successful in their striving for the admission of their work into the universities that 17 per cent of all Ph.D.'s granted in this country from 1951 to 1958 were given in education; they were half of all Ph.D.'s given in professional fields. Further, 34 per cent of all Ph.D.'s given in these years were given in professional fields, as against 9 per cent in the years from 1911 to 1920.[2] The M.A. has already become overwhelmingly a professional degree; the Ph.D. is following hard, with education leading all other subjects. In the next decade, Ph.D.'s in Education will almost certainly be granted to more people than in all of the physical sciences; they are already about equal in number to those in all of the social sciences. Education is a major—almost overwhelming—part of the American higher academic establishment. Indeed, at a conference called by the New England Board of Higher Education last year, a dean of education openly threatened the critics of education with use of the power which was rapidly passing from the hands of the rest of the university into those of education. Most of the Ph.D.'s, he said, would soon be in education and the rest of the academic profession would have to listen to them. I do not suppose this sentiment is widely shared, but the trend to which it calls attention is not to be ignored.

Education, as an academic subject, is primarily the study of schools; the preparation of schoolteachers and administrators has been the aim of departments of education. To belong to the profession of education, one must have something to do with schools. Just as in the business world, a man is asked whether he has ever

2. B. Berelson, *Graduate Education in the United States* (New York: McGraw-Hill, 1960), p. 37.

had to meet a payroll, so in the world of education he is asked whether he has ever actually taught school. People who have not done so are outsiders; they have not been set upon by parents, school boards, and inquisitorial senators. They have not been assailed by classroom air, thick and sweet with the smell of young America and dusty with chalk. They have not been the butt of academic jokes about departments of education. The people who have worked in schools and who have borne the brunt of the attacks which are made upon schoolteachers in this country and have had to cope with the unsolicited advice which everyone has to give about how and what to teach have had plenty of reason to be suspicious of outsiders. They may be pardoned for the belief that they have a sort of monopoly over the study of schools and the teaching and learning which takes place in them.

It is a part of professional ideology to insist that those who practice a profession are the only true and legitimate students of the branches of knowledge applied in it. Educationists do not believe it more than other professionals. Physicians have often been loath to accept biological research except on their own terms. Nurses, who are nowadays much concerned with research, are highly critical of research in which nurses are not the leading spirits. But the fact that education shares with other professions this jealousy does not make it a more sound or justifiable attitude.

The people most concerned, year in and year out, with an institution will of course have more to contribute to a study of it than any other group of people. They will have intimate knowledge of its inner working. They will sense its problems in their bones. But their very closeness to it makes many facts concerning it fall into their blind spot; and close identification is accompanied by vested interest, no matter how high the purposes of those involved.

There are problems which can be studied only by outsiders. Let us take an example. The changing of the name "teachers college" to simply "college," or "state college," prefixed by the name of a town or region of the state, has swept the country like a prairie fire. It is associated, of course, with a change to a more general curriculum leading to a bachelor's degree in subjects other than education (although I have yet to hear of a case in which the program in elementary education did not remain the central feature). One would expect that such a change of name and aim would be accompanied by internal conflicts of greater or less intensity between those who have long been attached to the institution and who have moved in the orbit of school systems and those newer people who come in primarily as college teachers and who have moved about or may move about in an orbit of liberal arts colleges. There is plenty of evidence that there is such conflict. Why should there not be? Changes in the aims, self-image, and public image of institutions are seldom achieved without conflict. It is in the interest of American education that attempts to change existing institutions to fit new needs and standards should be thoroughly understood. This can be done only by objective, comparative study with no holds barred. Yet I sat in a group composed largely of school people who claimed to be (and were) devoted to educational research and who condemned, out of hand, a proposal to study this change in a certain institution. Why? Because, they said, the change in name had already been made almost throughout the country until there are no teachers colleges left. Anthropologists speak of "name magic"! I should have thought that the generality of the change of name would have been a reason for studying its course and consequences. I could only conclude, since they were intelligent men, that they were protecting a vested interest, or perhaps they were merely trying to keep the peace. The people most involved in an institution often prefer not to have its most basic issues brought into the open. The protective device most often used is to deny the existence of the problem.

This is but one example. We, in this country, have an amazing variety of educational enterprises, initiated by various groups for a great variety of purposes. As time goes on, these institutions change in order to survive or in order to achieve new purposes. At the present time we are engaged in a great effort to make these institutions serve our aim, to achieve the national goals of equality of opportunity and high quality of achievement. In some respects our varied educational enterprises are becoming more alike as we pursue these goals; in others, they are becoming more diverse. Certain new enterprises are being initiated to provide education for special kinds of students; others, to provide certain kinds of education and training. Within many larger institutions there are special experimental programs. Incidentally, I have heard the proposal to study such an experiment called unscientific and of little use, because the experiment is unique and not statistically representative of American colleges. An odd conception of science! Many institutions once established for certain kinds of students and for certain kinds of education are being greatly changed to meet new demands. The internal functioning of these many institutions requires penetrating comparative study with particular attention to the problems of change and resistance to change. Their relations to each other require the same penetrating study, with special attention to the actual, as well as declared, division of labor among them. Study of these matters will require the best that we have in skill of observation and in theory and analysis of organizations.

As in all good comparative study of institutions, the concepts and methods of study will have to be drawn not merely from the particular kind of organization under study, but from organizations of many kinds and purposes. While the purposes for which an organization is established may have some effect on its form and functioning, they do not make an organization so peculiar that it can be fruitfully compared only with others devoted to the same purpose and studied only by people devoted to that purpose. Quite the contrary. One cannot gauge the effect of purposes unless one compares organizations of quite diverse purposes.

I say this so emphatically for two reasons. One is that, in this day of necessarily great specialization in the social sciences, there are people who devote their whole careers to study of one variety of institution—medical, business, governmental, educational. This specialization will fail of its goals if it is not countered and enriched by comparisons of organizations of various kinds.

The second reason is that professional specialization often leads to the *specialists' veto* in planning research and in granting the funds for it. By pointing to some small flaw or supposed naivete in a research plan, those who are specialists on the kind of organization concerned can often prevent the research from being done, thus protecting their own monopoly and perhaps preventing some important issue from being brought into the open. "How can these people, who obviously are naive about our organization, since they call our superintendent a manager, and don't know that we have five grades of help instead of four, possibly learn anything of value?"—so runs the reasoning. The ignorance and insight of the outsider do not coincide with those of the insider.

By combining what those inside can see and what they know, with what a comparative, objective student from outside can see, powerfully penetrating and useful studies of American educational institutions can be made. We must make them if we are to meet the educational problems of the country and of the great variety of individuals who compose it.

Although it is not my mandate to talk of fields other than education, I think it important to say that the relation of the inside professional and the outside researcher is essentially the same in all the many fields in our society in which there is a profession, or several professions, especially concerned with an institutional complex. We have many such institutional complexes, and the trend toward professionalism is strong in them. Objective, comparative study of them, with full access to their delicate and sometimes secret inner workings, is itself a delicate thing. It requires frankness between the parties concerned and some sort of responsible understanding in each case.

I have said, perhaps indirectly, that one of the things social scientists can offer to the field of education is study of the whole complement or system of educational institutions, study in which each is seen as a going concern with its own internal working constitution (relations and distribution of functions and power among the categories of people involved, including the pupils and students) and in which each, further, is seen in its relationship with other such institutions and with forces and institutions of other kinds.

One may speak of a basic ecology of education, of a complex of symbiotic relations among institutions. A teacher in a certain state university writes thus: "At ———— we have been particularly hard hit by the general improvement of standards in certain adjacent states. Our out-of-state enrollment runs about 25%, more than half from one state. Their turn-down rate swells their junior colleges—and we get lots of them."

The problem of selection of students in any institution is a function of the selection in other institutions. I do not say that this is a bad thing; only that we need studies of such relationships in metropolitan areas, states, and regions on which to base planning of our educational enterprises. Along with an ecology of selection of students by colleges and of colleges by students, we require one of college and university teachers in which we would learn more about the academic market, of the orbits in which academic people move. This would include also study of alternative careers in various lines of academic work.

But study of the ecology of education should go beyond the conventional schools and colleges, indeed beyond all kinds of schools and colleges. For, in spite of our colossal and growing rate of attendance at colleges, most of our young people do not get and probably do not want to get to college at all. Still, they learn things; they have skills, ideas, and knowledge. What skills, ideas, and knowledge? We do not know. Nor do we know how they learn what they do learn. Schools and colleges represent only part of the total teaching and learning which go on in society. Even in the schools, young people learn a great deal not taught by the teachers —some of it is, indeed, contrary to what the teachers teach, or believe they teach.

Sociologists, anthropologists, and social psychologists should actively study education in the broadest sense and in its total setting, not merely in the institutions ordinarily thought of as the educational system. Those institutions themselves we should study not merely in relation to one another, as suggested, but in relation to family, community, workshop, city streets, prisons, taverns, and the means of mass communication. And all this not merely in order that we may learn to bend these other institutions and groups to the will and aims of educational institutions; that might be one result. Feedback in the contrary direction might be an equally valuable result. This broader study should be done with a sense of history and with an eye to the natural history of institutions and of our society as a whole.

I have said little of the other topic—the inner constitution and workings of educational institutions. A large number of people are working on that problem and in a great variety of institutions. The social climates of high schools, the culture and perspectives of students in various kinds of undergraduate and professional schools, the levels and directions of student effort—these things are being studied. The literature is known to all who are likely to read these pages. Experiments are also being made in methods of teaching. We talk of the merits of lecturing as against discussion, of large and small classes, of teaching machines, of spoon-feeding as against putting students on their own. Yet we have almost no systematic observations of classroom behavior, of the interaction of teacher with pupils and students. Obviously, no teacher delivers ten or twelve or fifteen prepared and organized lectures a week, or even five. Teachers are not supermen. But probably most American college teachers do something in their classrooms for twelve or more hours a week. What is it they do? Do they mumble in their beards? Do they engage in chitchat? Do they really discuss subject matter and ideas with their students? In what combinations do they do these or other things? And how, for their part, do the students take part in what goes on? What skills have they developed for controlling what goes on in the classroom? And how is all of this affected by the teacher's conception of his job, and by what he considers to be the contingencies of his survival and advancement?

I am convinced that many American college teachers have

learned how to restrict production, their own and that of their students, as a means of survival, or at least as a means of leading a moderately peaceful existence. Most of our studies are based on the assumption that the teachers—and the administrators of the institutions in which they work—have as their goal an ever higher level of effort on the part of the students. If we were to study the interaction among administrators, teachers, pupils, and students, we might very well discover whole systems of checks upon the efforts of all concerned, a knot of fetters made tighter by the movements of all.

The study of this most basic of all educational activities, the goings-on in classrooms, combined with study of the other nuclei of interaction—of student with student, of teacher with teacher, administrator with administrator, and of each with the others and with various lay publics—is something which social scientists can do and which must eventually be done if we are to understand educational processes.

With it, I leave the matter, knowing that I have not given a catalog of the kinds of research which ordinarily go by the name of sociology of education.

COMMENTS   *James S. Coleman*

Mr. Hughes has given us an excellent catalog of research in the sociology of education. In giving this catalog, he has, I believe, come to the heart of the matter, for he has given examples of sociological research focused *on* the problems of education. How does he state the focus of this research? It "is something which social scientists can do, and which must eventually be done *if we are to understand educational processes.*" (Emphasis added.). The focus is upon educational processes, not upon adding to our sociological knowledge.

That this focus is a crucial matter is evident to anyone who reads a sociological journal or even a sociological article in an educational journal. Papers abound which use schools as a convenient locus of research—research directed to winning applause from within the discipline of sociology. For, above all, disciplines are tight "in-groups" of those who award status—and jobs—to one another. As long as sociologists and psychologists look wholly within for their rewards of status, jobs, and the like, they will not be concerned with understanding educational processes, and what light they may throw upon educational processes will be purely accidental.

It is for this reason that Mr. Hughes's focus of attention upon educational processes for themselves alone is refreshing, but I think also misleading. For who is going to do this research? Not the academic sociologists concerned with status in their own discipline. (Here I except Mr. Hughes and a few others, for in his work as well as his words, he has shown an interest in understanding the processes central to that institution he is studying—whether it be a school or a factory.)

The point is this: we must decide first of all whether or not the study of educational problems is an appropriate focus of interest within a university. If it is, then the implications are clear: there must be men whose principal focus of interest is the theory and practice of education. Otherwise, the wrong problems are solved: a psychologist uses a set of students as convenient guinea pigs; a sociologist studies schools to learn about how status systems operate; an administrative theorist finds schools a convenient organization to advance his knowledge of administration. Now these are all important questions, but the answers they produce feed into a different discipline and seldom aid the problems of education. The psychologist or sociologist tips his hat to the school, says "Thank you, ma'am," and takes his findings back to his own discipline to show to his colleagues.

The problem, then, is a problem which Mr. Hughes has dealt with here and throughout his work: the organization of effort—the appropriate organization of effort to solve educational problems. To say that the present organization is not appropriate, as I think Mr. Walton implied at the outset of this conference, is something with which I can heartily agree; to take the next step, and suppose that creation of a separate discipline will organize effort in these directions, takes, I think, precisely the wrong path. An academic discipline becomes wholly self-contained and self-admiring. It is the most narcissistic form of social organization, a form appropriate only to those areas of knowledge for which few demands come from the outside. But, as Mr. Hughes suggests, education and medicine are activities, or arts, which must be *practiced,* activities which daily provide criteria of success or failure. These external demands discourage narcissistic contemplation and focus talents toward the solution of problems. They require an organization of effort very different from the self-admiring disciplines, though one which is totally selfish in using these disciplines for its own ends.

Should there be a discipline of space vehicles in universities? Probably not. But if space vehicles are to be built, it is not enough to count on the intrinsic individual interests of physicists, engineers, and others to get a space vehicle built. It simply will not come about. There must be some appropriate organization of effort which will bring together the necessary talents and focus those talents on the specific problem of space vehicles.

What, then, is the appropriate organization of effort if educational processes are to be understood? It may be something wholly outside the universities. It may be something akin to the transformation which occurred with medical schools. Modern medicine in the United States did not come about by the transformation of a medical school into a general college or a university (as is occurring today with the teachers college); it came about by making them more concerned with fundamental problems of medicine, not less. It came about by bringing research from scientific disciplines into the medical school, but *on its own terms*—that is, to focus upon medicine, upon problems of bodily functioning and malfunctioning. Perhaps, then, education is just putting the finishing touches on a move in the wrong direction—transforming its own institutions into general colleges, rather than into institutions for research into educational processes.

I am not suggesting that this *is* the appropriate organization of effort. I am suggesting, rather, that, as Mr. Hughes says, education is an art, not a discipline, and that its welfare will depend on the ingenuity of its practitioners in focusing the efforts of a number of disciplines to work on *its* problems.

VIII

The Nature and the Uses
of the Study of Education

JAMES DEESE

SUCH IMPORTANT institutions of our society as law, finance, and religion are quite properly the sources of scholarly activity, research, and teaching. The teaching is necessary so that some of the formal knowledge useful to the managing of these institutions can be passed on to the young. The scholarly activity and research are part of the civilized interest in the study of man and his works. Thus, in modern society, money begets—in addition to evil— economics and graduate schools of business administration. Law begets lawyers but also legal and political theory. Religion produces both theology and seminarians.

The institution of education requires teachers and, in addition, places for the selection and training of those teachers. These places are the schools and colleges of education. Some of these are also centers for the study of schooling itself. It is this conjunction of teaching and research that provides the academic setting for the discipline of education.

This combination of teaching how to teach and research on teaching is a sensible arrangement despite its abuses, since it provides or should provide a meeting of new ideas about schooling and the teachers who will ultimately be concerned with the practical implications of those ideas. Thus, the school of education is

163

a center of both pure and applied research, and a conjunction of the training of teachers and research upon schooling is the prevailing rule in such institutions.

It is not necessary, of course, that the study of any social institution be so directly associated with the training of the professional people who manage the institution. Many social institutions are studied in centers entirely divorced from teaching. The traditional place for the pure study of social institutions is the liberal arts faculty, whose students are not supposed to be trained for any particular profession or craft.

I hope to be able to show that the study of schooling is, at least in some important respects, a social science and that its study need not be ancillary to professional training of teachers. It is in many ways as pure a social science as the study of economics or psychology. In other respects it is not, and it is necessary to examine these in order to understand education's position within the social sciences. Because education is somewhat unusual as a social science and because of tradition, as well as practical demands, the study of schooling within the setting of the school of education is established, and I believe that it is not necessarily an evil arrangement. Because it is not widely accepted that schools of education should be places for pure research, some argument about the nature of education as a social science is necessary.

In a developed, urban, and overpopulated society such as ours, every aspect of human life is the subject of some learned inquiry. Even so prosaic an enterprise as poultry raising cannot be left to the vagaries of unaided nature. There are departments of poultry husbandry in the great state universities staffed by professors of poultry husbandry who do research on the problems of raising and marketing chickens, turkeys, and ducks.

Despite the good services provided by such departments, I think that it is reasonable to say that they do not constitute academic disciplines. This judgment does not imply that these departments are without value within the university. Most applied sciences have some role in society, and some disciplines that have traditionally been regarded as applied, such as education, make important contributions to pure knowledge. Society needs certain of the applied disciplines, and they are appropriate to the traditions and purposes of many American universities. Even among those critics of education who regard it, at best, as a purely applied study, I believe there are not many who would want to banish it altogether.

Part of the question of the nature of education is whether or not it is a pure or applied discipline. In order to separate the applied disciplines from the pure studies we need some criteria. These criteria should clearly designate such programs as poultry husbandry as applied, and they should tell us whether education is to be classed among the applied or among the pure disciplines. Or, since many subjects are mixed in character, education among these, these criteria should help us describe the ways in which the study of any subject is both pure and applied.

One criterion that differentiates the purely practical sciences from the academic disciplines is the extent to which inquiry contributes to the abstract understanding of some human, natural, or philosophic problem. This criterion would be met when the solution to some problem or the consideration of some idea has implications beyond the problem or the idea investigated. Many worthy scientific enterprises are not concerned with abstract questions or matters of pure knowledge, but concerned with rules of procedure designed to maximize the likelihood of some explicit outcome. A treatment of such a question as the economics of schooling could be a purely practical matter—the best procedure for the fiscal management of schools. Or, on the other hand, it could raise a general problem about the measurement of the utility of social services. In general, those problems which do not concern specific ends are the problems of pure inquiry, though as I shall mention later, applied problems sometimes raise general and abstract questions.

It is nevertheless evident that many of the problems which occupy the attention of persons in schools or departments of education are purely practical questions. This is necessarily the case. We cannot quarrel with such a necessity without endangering belief in some of the principles which give rise to the social support of schooling. We may quarrel with the competence of the investigation of particular practical problems in education, and we may even quarrel with the relative importance of some of the problems chosen for investigation, but not many of us would want to quarrel with the need for some practical study of educational problems.

Because so many of the investigations that have come out of the study of practical problems in education are trivial, there is no little temptation to class the study of education with the least significant and important of the practical sciences which find their way into the various curricula of American universities. Such a temptation should be avoided, since the study of education is in nearly all respects like the study of other important institutions of society. To ask questions about schooling is to ask questions about human nature, about social organization, and about values. The study of education raises questions of general intellectual importance.

It seems so evident to me that the study of schooling, of teaching and learning, is as fundamental as the study of money or law that it is almost unnecessary to raise any question about it. It is perhaps because of the cloud of criticism over the discipline of education that the question arises at all. Except among certain obscurantists, however, the main force of that criticism is seen to fall upon the competence of those who practice the study of education, not upon the discipline itself. The more fundamental study of education exists alongside of and sometimes as part of the study of the practical problems faced by the educators. This situation has created some confusion about the nature of education and is in part responsible for the widely held opinion that education is not a fundamental academic study. A word of comment on this situation is in order.

In the years following World War II it was fashionable to point out the difference between basic and applied science and to emphasize the really important scientific achievements that come out of basic research. At that time this point was made as an attempt to persuade the various governmental agencies responsible for the fiscal support of research to allot a greater share of the available funds to basic research. The distinction between the pure and the applied can be overdrawn, however. The criteria which differentiate the particulars of basic research from those of applied research vary from discipline to discipline. It is often very hard to tell what is basic and what is applied. Even when the most general criterion, generality itself, is applied, the distinction does not always seem to lead to the right results. Often, purely practical problems generate questions of great theoretical and general importance. Research upon applied problems does feed back to basic science, though not so spectacularly as in the reverse case. Often, we must admit, in the social sciences pure research is trivial because theories themselves are concerned with trivial questions.

A close interdependence between pure and applied research is characteristic of the social sciences. I think this is because of the great importance, at the present stage of development, of empirical investigation in the social sciences. Sound choice of empirical problems in the social sciences depends upon an intuitive, implicit knowledge on the part of the investigator of what is important of the number of things which are possible to investigate. The social scientist faces a very large number of problems to be investigated, and the importance of his research is probably more dependent upon the excellence of his choice among these than upon any other single factor.

Nowhere is the distinction between the purely basic and the purely applied more likely to lead to pernicious effects than in the study of education. Here, more than in other social sciences, the sound choice of a problem depends upon a close, firsthand knowledge of the conditions to be investigated. An insistence upon separation of pure and applied study leads to the emphasis, on the one hand, upon the trivial practical questions of the day and, on the other hand, to emphasis upon sterile academic problems generated from sterile academic theories. Academic questions in education are often sterile because they are of no general social importance and lead to no implications, practical or otherwise, except, perhaps, for further research upon sterile problems. I believe this state of affairs has been characteristic of much of the effort to study theories of learning in the educational context.

Education, in company with other social sciences, is by nature both a basic and applied discipline. Because there is mutual support and because the subject matter of education requires some concrete experience with the social realities of schooling, no strict line can profitably be drawn between the pure and applied aspects of the study. Suffice it to say that the nature of the subject matter insures opportunity for significant study uncontrolled by the demands for application.

There is another characteristic of the study of education which makes it a somewhat unusual social science. It is a characteristic typical of many disciplines that are largely applied in nature. Most basic disciplines have a body of method. Sometimes the method is well defined and specific, and sometimes it is only an intuitive knowledge of the way to proceed. Education, in company with most applied disciplines, does not have a unique body of method that serves to define its study. It relies on the methods in the traditions of other disciplines.

This may appear to be an astonishing statement in view of the frequency with which educators talk about "research methodology." There is, however, nothing unique about the methods of investigation employed by the educators. There are traditional techniques and methods of approach that have grown up as the result of special problems faced in the study of education. It is true that some important modifications of general principles of empirical investigation have come into prominence in the context of educational research. This is especially true in statistical analysis and experimental design. These principles, however, are as applicable to the study of agriculture or psychology as they are to education, and they are modifications of methods general to sciences which employ statistical analysis.

Within each discipline there is a tradition of method. These traditional methods differ as much from one another as the disciplines themselves differ. All intellectual enterprises make use of the common body of analytic technique and knowledge embodied in applied mathematics, logic, grammar, and the analysis of language. In addition, however, each special study is characterized by its own particular methods, and these methods define the unique contributions to knowledge made by that study.

Students of educational problems make use of the techniques and traditions of particular disciplines from which their studies derive. Thus, educational psychologists do about as many things as psychologists as a whole do. They use the technique of personality assessment and ability testing, and they rely for experimental techniques and hypotheses upon the body of psychological research at large. Educational psychologists contribute their share to the body of psychological knowledge, but they do so as psychologists, not as educators.

Much of contemporary theory of testing and the study of special abilities is in the hands of the educational psychologists. This, however, is an historical accident and by no means the result of particular skills developed by the study of education. The educational psychologist frequently publishes the results of his studies in journals devoted to larger areas of psychology. When he publishes in the more general educational journals, *The Harvard Educational Review* or *The Teachers College Record,* he is more likely to write as a psychologist talking to educators than as an educator among educators.

The dependency of educational psychology upon psychology as a whole can be seen by a casual inspection of the names of individuals who are Fellows of the Division on Educational Psychology of the American Psychological Association. A surprisingly large number of these individuals have appointments only in psychology departments. While their research activities are in educational psychology, they do not have appointments in schools or departments of education. A larger number, perhaps the majority of Fellows of this division, have joint appointments in psychology and education. Thus, educational psychologists are little more than psychologists with special interests. I doubt very much if one would find the reverse of this situation. That is to say, it would be hard to find individuals who were first and foremost educators in the psychology departments of the universities.

I do not know in any firsthand way, but I suspect that much the same would be true of educational sociology. I suspect that, in technique and ideas, educational sociologists are more sociologists than educators studying a particular problem. The methods and outlook of these individuals are sociological in nature, and they write as sociologists.

I think much the same must be true of the best efforts in educational history. I am not altogether certain that I know what precisely is meant by the phrase "historical method." One hears the phrase, however, and I am reasonably certain that it refers to something. The method of the historian is likely to be less formal, more intuitive, and less subject to textbook description, but nonetheless real. One has only to examine history written by a historian and compare it with history written by an educator or a psychologist to be convinced of the influence of historical method. Any satisfactory attempt to relate the institution of schooling to intellectual and social histories at large relies on the tradition and method of the professional historian.

The best histories of education are in the tradition of history, though they may be written by individuals whose primary university affiliations are with departments of education. They owe little or nothing beyond subject matter to the discipline of education. Thus in history, as in sociology and psychology, the study of schooling provides problems but no unique method nor any particular intellectual tradition.

Education is a discipline with a central object of study but with no unity of tradition or method. Perhaps it is this lack of unity of tradition that has produced the idols of scientism, professionalism, and obscurantism. In any event, when the professors of education contribute to the sum of human knowledge, they do so very often as practitioners of other traditions applied to the problems of schooling. In this sense education fails to meet the requirements of a basic discipline. It has no tradition or method and hence no intellectual viewpoint of its own. Because, however, the subject matter is a fundamental one, the study of education should not be left to those whose interests are solely in the practical and the immediate.

Because of the lack of a tradition in method, almost necessarily the study of basic problems in education is done by individuals whose backgrounds and academic preparation vary. In no small measure, educators depend for method upon the contributing disciplines upon which they draw. This fact implies that there should be a steady and large infusion of individuals from other fields into education. Historians, psychologists, philosophers, and linguists whose interests draw them to the topics of schooling need to be encouraged and rewarded for the study of education.

At the same time, the professors of education, the scholars who study the problems of schooling, should not be drawn entirely from the ranks of those who have their backgrounds in other fields. Nor should the study of education be left to fragmented efforts in other disciplines. Historians and sociologists who study education should know and understand each other. It is as important to relate the history of education to educational psychology as it is to relate the history of education to the history of technology. The problems which deserve attention from across disciplinary boundaries are exciting. I can think of no more worthwhile project for a historian of education than to tackle the question of transfer of training. To do so, however, such a historian must be steeped in education and social history and, in addition, know something about contemporary thought in educational psychology and the psychology of learning.

I do not intend to discuss the question of graduate training in education, but a word on this subject is necessary to avoid the possible implication that graduate work in education be entirely abandoned in favor of work in the other special fields. This should not be done for several reasons. For one thing, some students of education should have the firsthand intuitive knowledge that comes from actual work in the school systems. These people come to the scholarly study of education from direct experience with the subject. Second, there must be within the discipline of education a large body of individuals who can bring together and relate the methods and traditions of the special fields that contribute to the study of education. These are people who stand at the center of the field of inquiry, "generalists" in education, if you like. Third, some problems, problems in curriculum, administration, and the training of teachers are so close to applied studies that they cannot be considered in any other setting but education.

One implication of these views about education should be made explicit. It is that all students of education should have a thorough background in some one discipline useful to the study of education and a fair acquaintance with some of the other disciplines that contribute to education. This makes rigorous and difficult demands upon graduate students in education, but these are made by their chosen field of inquiry.

Though the study of education involves no unique tradition or method that serves to differentiate it from the other social sciences, its concern with an aspect of society so highly institutionalized makes the contributions of those who have worked in the schools useful. Those with some direct experience of teaching in the public schools serve to pull together the separate strands in the discipline of education. They are the individuals who can understand the jargon of special methods, who can see relationships between such things as the theory of transfer of training and the development of an industrial society, who, in a word, can contribute the problems of education.

I have implied that the study of education is primarily a social science. It is, of course, concerned with moral and philosophical problems often eschewed by social scientists. Most students of education, however, are concerned with the facts of schooling and theories about those facts. Thus an important issue in the study of education concerns the uses and limitations of empirical information about schooling. To deal with the nature of education, it is necessary to examine the kinds of factual information that can be gathered about learning and teaching and the uses to which these may be put.

There are two points of view from which we may look at the uses of the study of education, though one of these is by overwhelming use and importance the more usual one. We may, and usually do, consider the ends achieved by the society which supports academic inquiry into schooling. In addition, however, we may consider the ends achieved by those who are the students of education. This may seem to be a curious question to consider, but it is, I believe, an important determiner of the excellence of the study of education.

To some extent at least I hope that educators study their subject out of curiosity. At the same time I think that a curiosity about some aspect of schooling is not something that comes easily to the college student. It is very likely the result of some particular and quite specific experience with education. It may come sometimes from an interest in and study of one of the disciplines that lends its methods to education, or it may come from direct experience with schooling, usually as a teacher, but surely on occasion at least, as a pupil.

Given the best motivation, an interest in ideas and in knowing, it is most certainly accidental contingencies and unique characteristics of personality that lead an academically bent individual into the study of education. Money, social origins and aspirations, job tenure have all been identified in empirical surveys as things which appear to push individuals into the study of education. These are not necessarily bad or damaging to the intellectual climate of the discipline. They are intellectually irrelevant, but they exert profound influence upon all academic disciplines, not the least upon the study of education. To the extent that education is a basic academic discipline, however, nothing further than curiosity need be relevant. The scholar and society generally agree in the broadest sense upon the ends of academic inquiry, and this is enough.

The goal of the study of any problem is to produce understanding of that problem. This is an easy enough principle to state (and to agree with), but an interpretation of exactly what it means leads to difficulties. There is not universal agreement on the criteria of understanding, nor should there be, given the variety of things into which the human mind inquires. Concern with the criteria of understanding has been a major philosophical activity of the past sixty years or so, and in the empirical social sciences that concern has led to some rather explicit methodological principles.

Many of the social sciences, particularly those in which investigators gather data in a form analogous to the methods of the natural sciences, have developed excellent and stringent, though by no means sufficient, criteria to apply to the achievement of understanding. These criteria have been variously stated, but in their baldest form they can be stated as the prediction of new events from principles derived from the study of past events, and the control of events by control over those variables that cause them. Prediction and control are objective criteria that tell us that some measure of understanding has been achieved.

These are powerful tests of understanding. They are so powerful that they have come to be regarded by many social scientists as the ends of knowledge. Sciences governed completely by these principles are applied sciences, sciences the ends of which are practical. Consequently, if there is any validity at all in the distinction between pure and applied study, prediction and control cannot be ends in themselves for pure inquiry.

Some of the questions examined by the students of education lend themselves to test by these criteria. Even in these cases, the

criteria themselves need to be regarded only as tests of the degree
to which some particular problem is understood. More than this is
the province of the student of applied education. It is, however,
difficult to apply these tests to all intellectual inquiry centering
about schooling. They are difficult to apply to history or to the study
of the individual personality. The study of personality or history is
individualistic and intuitive. Predictive implications may be derived
from such study, but only at the considerable risk of failure. Personality theory, more often than not, is a kind of attitude which orients
one towards psychological problems, not a theory in the generally
accepted scientific sense.

I use the study of personality as an example, and I mean it to
illustrate the difficulty of applying so particular a criterion as prediction to the question of understanding. The function of the study
of personality is to provide a background of experience against
which we may judge and evaluate what is happening to individual human beings. We do not use the material of study to predict particular outcomes with a specified level of probability, but we
can use such material to establish a range of possible outcomes.
These let us know what the reasonable limits of expectation are.

I do not mean to imply that the lack of predictability in the study
of the individual or in the study of certain aspects of social systems is something metaphysical or inherent in the freedom of the
individual human mind or the human will. It is simply that the limitations of the methods available to us and the inherent difficulties
in the subject matter do not allow us to apply the ordinary canons
of induction with anything like a specifiable degree of accuracy. We
may use historical material or case studies to predict outcomes with
free abandon, but such prediction is intuitive, and it is usually
based on preconception rather than inductive evidence. When it
is inductive, it is based upon single instances which embody unique
circumstances not likely to occur again.

The case method and the historical method provide poor foundation for inductive inference. Because the events that make up any
considerable narrative about an individual or about a society are

always but a part of the total possible narrative and because that narrative itself is a complicated causal chain, it can be nothing more than a description of a set of unique circumstances. We may know with some degree of accuracy the outcome of a relation between a pair of events in such a narrative, but we are usually reduced to ignorance when we try to examine all the possible interactions between these events and others that have occurred in the same narrative or before the narrative has begun. Any prediction is based upon the identification of some segment of the narrative with some events that have been studied by laboratory or other techniques outside of the narrative setting that makes up the case history. The use of such identification to make predictions is risky because the laboratory or controlled observations that gave rise to the prediction do not take into account the interactions with other events that occur in the narrative of the individual case.

One of the most successful and highly developed examples of the application of empirical study to individual histories occurs in psychological testing. All students of testing, however, are aware of the great discrepancies between the well-specified errors of measurement obtainable from normative information and the actual errors of measurement in individual cases. The outcome of a testing program may be used to establish, with specified limits of precision, what we are to expect from a population of individuals. Thus, the city of Baltimore can predict with considerable accuracy the distribution of abilities within its school system from year to year, and it may, by the use of social and ecological information, predict changes in these distributions from time to time and from area to area within the city. In theory the same knowledge about distributions should yield the limits of prediction for individual cases.

The results of even the best testing procedures must be used with "clinical judgment" in individual cases, however. If not, some information must be discarded. Clinical judgment means, I think, that the user of the test does not rely completely on the statistical information about the test but reserves the right to consider the statistical information in the light of individual facts known from the case history. It can be argued, of course, that the clinical judgment itself should be based upon inductive inference, and therefore, if we had the right information, it should be possible to outguess clinical judgment by statistical information. The fact is that we do not at present gather the right information, and—given the great range of possibilities in individual histories—it is unlikely that we can do so in the near future. The problem of prediction from any appreciable fraction of the range of individual circumstances is simply one of size. We cannot get enough statistical information about any particular combination of unique circumstances to make a distribution suitable for inductive inference. Even if the information were available, it would be impractical to process it by current techniques.

This example is meant to illustrate that the limitation in ways of gathering knowledge at the present time makes it impossible to apply the canons of inductive inference to all of the problems in so complicated a human system as the schools. It is not possible to experiment with histories, nor is it possible to compare histories which differ only in some particular detail as a means of testing out information about particular causal relations in complicated systems.

Even when it is possible to study parts of complicated systems experimentally, or by some other powerful empirical method, the great number of possible interactions between causative events makes the application of analytic empirical techniques difficult and liable to errors of oversimplification. Consider the problem of experimentally comparing the outcome of different procedures used by teachers in classrooms.

The effectiveness of any classroom procedure depends upon a large number of things, some of which are readily identifiable and others of which probably are not. Certainly a procedure depends upon the teacher who administers it. This is not an idle statement, but one which can be backed up by countless studies of educational practices, studies which show an interaction between method and teachers. In addition to the teacher, a classroom will have anywhere from twenty to fifty pupils (the number itself being an important variable), all of whom interact with each other and with the teacher. Each of these individuals provides a source of unique interaction with procedural differences. Thus, even though we may find an average difference between any particular procedures under study, we know by the results of our study that it will be modified to great degrees by the individuals who employ the procedures compared. Furthermore, these collections of twenty to fifty children will vary from locale to locale and from time to time in ways that will be relevant to the procedural differences.

Given this situation, it is not surprising that the literature on experimental variations in classroom procedures is disappointing. The mean effects are small and frequently applicable to particular situations only at the risk of destroying the small mean effect. I do not think that the experimental study of the classroom is hopeless or doomed to failure, but we ought not to expect too much from the traditional experimental comparisons. If we are to apply the outcomes of scientific studies of the individual and such collections of individuals as occur in the classroom, we must in most instances content ourselves with small average effects, and, in all probability, we must use some judgment in applying the information.

Information about average effects is necessary to the efficient management of large social institutions such as the schools or the military establishment. Thus, despite their limitations, the large objective testing programs of the schools are useful, and by now they are probably necessary. Such programs cannot be applied to individuals in the same way that they are applied in the mass, since the information available to us in single cases will lead us to modify the objective, statistical interpretation of results in the light of what else we know about the individual or particular school being considered.

Studies of procedural change and programs of testing have, in the past, been most efficient when the role of individual histories is minimized. Some new approaches give promise of much closer approximation to control over the factors responsible for individual histories and hence much greater control in individual cases. These are the approaches based upon the notion of programming, and the best known current examples are the teaching machines. Because programs are flexible, have large numbers of alternatives, and make decisions about alternatives in particular cases—decisions based upon the state of the individual at that moment—they can approximate the functions of the teacher or some other individual who makes decisions about what to do from moment to moment in the classroom. Furthermore, they can make these decisions upon some fixed, error-free criterion. Within some domains, the concept of programming will extend the uses of empirical information in education. At present, the teaching machines themselves appear to be most useful in the teaching of skills which have inherent logical structures, particularly hierarchical structures.

Prediction and control, then, are excellent criteria of understanding and they also provide us with some of the uses of understanding. They are not always easy to apply, however, and I think little is gained by pretending that they are. It is futile to issue promissory notes about the future applications of the scientific study of education. The scientific study of education can be justified on intrinsic grounds, on the return to the investigator himself and in terms of the gains to a society that places a value upon the understanding of social and natural problems. Indeed, I suspect that belief in utopian promises about the prediction and control of behavior has been in part responsible for some of the adverse criticism of the study of education and the social sciences generally. The scientific canons of prediction and control have led some people into the belief that all knowledge about a social system can and should be applied, and the sooner the better. Because any part of the social system studied scientifically is no more than a more or less arbitrary segment of the whole, the possible interactions of that part with other, unstudied parts of the whole are ignored. Furthermore, an easy reliance on scientific control leads us to neglect inquiry into the ends that are served by controlled change. I do not mean to imply that experimentalism and instrumentalism are bad, but I would like to suggest that we be a bit more tentative and skeptical in the application of the empirical information we have and that we be not so quick to demand that all information about man and his society meet the requirements of prediction and control.

What are the uses, then, of the study of education? I think we must answer that in some respects they are the same as the uses of any other academic discipline and, therefore, in important particulars should be distinguished from the uses of poultry husbandry or other applied disciplines. This is not to say, of course, that the study of education should not also be an applied study. The student of education, however, need not ask whether he is increasing the effectiveness of the schools or whether he is engaged in research designed to channel the activities of the schools into a more useful course. A study of education need not justify itself on the basis of any contribution it makes to the control over the outcomes of education, though this may be a useful by-product of that study.

It remains a basic supposition, I suppose, of the social support of any scholarly or scientific enterprise that study, investigation, and scholarship will, in the long run, increase our ability to adjust the human condition to the demands of the world in which we live and to do this by explicit and rational means. However vague this supposition may be, society does not support scholarly activity simply because of the intrinsic rewards to the scholar. It turns out, probably for social and psychological reasons that themselves deserve study, that society is best rewarded in the long run when the scholar is left to pursue his own basic interests. It is in this respect that the study of education has been a conspicuous failure. There are too few professional students of education who follow their own work untrammeled by the demands for specific results. Too often, the hardheaded criteria for empirical investigation, pre-

diction and control, have agreed with the demands for quick re-
turns in education. Educators, in company with many social scientists, have been too eager to see the results of their scholarly work
embedded in social change.

The pressure for application is in good measure the result of the
expectation that the study of education will, in the unelegant but
singularly appropriate phrase, pay off. This pressure, accompanied
by the scholar's own interests in further large-scale tests of his
notions has resulted in a tendency to rush into action with some
new device, principle, or method when a more leisurely consideration in the atmosphere of the ivory tower would be more appropriate.

In simple systems, the tendency to introduce specific and isolated
change is not so objectionable. In physical systems, in which a
localized set of events is controlled by a limited number of variables, there is little effect outside of the system when change is
introduced, save, of course, when the effect is amplified by man's
social structure. Thus, the consequences of change can be contained. No matter how carefully possible outside effects are considered, however, the study of an isolated social system necessarily
neglects some conditions which function in a real society. It is impossible to effect a social change in isolation.

At one time I was convinced that a detailed and exhaustive study
would show that the whole secondary educational system in the
United States could be made more efficient by cutting off the
twelfth year. Thus public school education would be terminated at
the end of the eleventh grade. Suppose that a careful and thorough
investigation, supported by an analysis of the aims of education in
American society, were to suggest that such a scheme would be
feasible and would result in correction of such diverse conditions
as delinquency rates, failure rates in college, the excessive length of
time in study for the learned professions, and so on. However
carefully such a scheme would be considered, it is probable that
unforeseen circumstances would appear in any application of the

principle. Perhaps it would be in the form of an alarming increase in birth rate, or perhaps a decrease. One could go on enumerating such possibilities almost endlessly and still be sure that some were left unconsidered.

Such a scheme may indeed be useful to society; I do not mean to imply that we should cease all social action because we cannot foresee all outcomes. The more we know, however, the more consequences we can foresee. In a word, we know better what we are doing. Society, in the long run, is benefited by careful consideration of practical action as much as the social sciences suffer from hasty commitments to it.

The scholar should be the one to resist most firmly the pressure to precipitate action. I think one way that resistance may be stiffened is to make certain that scholarly activity is its own intrinsic reward. Intrinsic reward to scholarly or scientific work occurs less often in the study of education than it should. In education, the scholar is likely to yield to the pressure for application because of the emphasis upon results in the study of education; research is frequently bought and paid for on the basis of a specific problem. Moreover, I suspect that a lack of genuine intellectual curiosity about the subject matter results in many students of education substituting social action for the rewards of pure research. Finally, we all know that many Ph.D. dissertations are done (and not a few studies from mature scholars) not out of intrinsic interest but by extrinsic demands for publication and the accompanying notoriety. The inevitable result is a mass of busy-work.

I have tried to argue that education is a social science as well as an applied discipline. It is a somewhat unusual social science, though probably not absolutely unique, in that it has no unique tradition of method of its own. It makes use of a variety of traditions, traditions associated with psychology, philosophy, history, economics, and the study of social institutions. It provides a well-defined subject matter—schooling—which is a fundamental activity of civilized society and which, indeed, may be a direct outcome of human nature.

Because so much of the vitality of research and scholarly work on the subject of schooling depends upon traditions outside of the discipline of education, education cannot afford to be free of the other social sciences. There should, therefore, be a continuous infusion of individuals from other disciplines into the study of education. Since education has a central core of subject matter, however, it also needs an intellectual tradition, not of method but of first-hand acquaintance with the subject matter, a tradition that can be maintained by individuals whose training and career is entirely within the subject matter of education.

The study of education should satisfy both the demands of the society that supports the study and the needs of the scholar who pursues the investigation. Perhaps one of the great deficiencies of the study of education is the lack of intrinsic interest on the part of those who practice it. The extrinsic demands of society and the devotion to the concept of research—any kind of research—as a way of satisfying society's demands appear to be a substitute for intrinsic interest on the part of the student of education.

Scholarly activity is almost necessarily inefficient. No one can tell what kind of activity will in the long run be most satisfying to the investigator and those who support him. It is the inefficiency and uncertainty of scholarly work that makes the ivory tower so valuable a place. Educators are too often to be found in the marketplace selling their wares rather than in the ivory tower. They should be in the marketplace frequently enough as observers and perhaps as buyers, but not so often as sellers. The temptation provided by the rewards of action are many, and the current pressure on public education has increased them. If we cannot herd a large number of the educators into the ivory tower, perhaps we ought at least to press for such a sanctuary for those among the students of education who want one. One of the first steps in providing such a refuge is to recognize the claims of education as a pure discipline.

COMMENTS *Robert M. W. Travers*

A central thesis of Professor Deese's paper is that those engaged in research on educational problems are professional persons with major ties to areas outside education, who do not have strong ties to the educational profession. A brief examination of this thesis is in order at this time, for two reasons. First, there is the well-known tendency for colleges and schools of education to employ those who have had public school experience. In some teacher-training institutions this is a requirement for employment. The result of this practice is to exclude from these institutions persons with a bent for research. The second major factor is that such institutions are under considerable pressure to perform the practical tasks related to the training of teachers and heavy teaching loads are the rule. When these institutions receive a small financial windfall the pressure is on the administration to cut the teaching and supervisory loads rather than to expand research facilities. Some years ago the dean of a college of education in a large state university was concerned to develop research in his college. His faculty on being asked to write their views on such a development, observed that if money was available, there were more important things to do with it than sponsor research. My sympathies are both with the dean and with his overburdened staff in this matter.

The remedies for this situation lie in two directions. The insistence upon staffing colleges of education with holders of teaching certificates or with public school experience reflects the growth of professionalism in education, but it also reflects a trend in professional education which is the opposite of the trend in many other professional fields. Medical schools, for example, draw their faculties from many varied disciplines, and a large percentage of the teaching staff are scientists who have never qualified to practice medicine. A reversal in the policy of teacher-training institutions might produce a new atmosphere in schools of education congenial to the development of research and might even lead to the development of a discipline in the area itself. If schools of education were to include on their staffs more persons thoroughly expert in related disciplines, the training of the new generation of professors of education would place greater emphasis on the mastery of one or more of these disciplines. Deese suggests in his paper that all students of education should have a thorough background in one discipline related to education, but this is unlikely to occur until most colleges of education have changed their staffing practices.

I generally endorse the discussion of pure and applied research presented by Deese and also his refusal to accept the criteria of prediction and control as the sole criterion of scientific advance. Much of what passes for research in education results in some small measure of prediction and sometimes some degree of control. These outcomes appear to me to be necessary conditions for understanding, but not sufficient conditions. The teacher who predicts that pupils who have slingshots are to be watched as troublemakers, or who controls the playful behavior of pupils by shouting, has not achieved a state in any way resembling that of scientific understanding, though he has achieved some degree of prediction and control. This is a point which many of my colleagues in education seem to have missed. Practices based on folklore may be valid but they do not rest on a body of scientific information, on an organized body of knowledge, but simply on a collection of odds and ends of information. Knowledge which produces law of wide generality is based on research of a systematic, programmatic type which builds systems of related concepts and variables; but educational research has not had this characteristic except as it has been pursued by persons who have come to it from related disciplines. Such research, conducted from the periphery of education, has often had little meaning to those engaged in practical educational activities, who expect it to achieve prediction and control at an early stage. What is not realized by these practically-oriented persons is that prediction and control emerge from scientific work often rather late in its development. Laws of high generality are a product of prolonged research effort rather than single-shot inquiries. One is reminded of the fact that after Newton postulated a universal gravitational constant, a hundred years elapsed before it was finally measured by the great Cavendish and Newton's equations could finally be put to use. I suspect that educators have an impatience in such matters which they share with most other practically-oriented men.

Within the field of professional education there is another attitude or point of view which interferes with the development of scientific inquiry. This is the position that research should be undertaken by first identifying problems for which solutions are urgently needed and then planning research to solve these problems. On the surface the approach has a certain logic to it which makes it seductively attractive, but the fact is that rarely in the history of scientific inquiry has this procedure had any success. This is the approach of the alchemist. An urgent need for gold suggested to the political lords that this problem might be solved by employing alchemists who would conduct research on the transformation of the base metals into the valuable ones. History has clearly shown how profitless this procedure turned out to be. While the alchemists were pursuing their investigation of "important" problems, men like Galileo were accused of studying trivial matters. In this field, as in most others, the direct investigation of complex but socially important matters turned out to be the wrong approach. My impression is that the head-on attack on important practical problems has had as little success in education as it has had in chemistry and physics. At least, one cannot point to any notable accomplishments at this time, but one can point to laboratory inquiries into problems which on the surface appear to be of only academic interest, but which have had great impact on education. The research of the late E. L. Thorndike is an admirable illustration of the latter. Despite this lesson of history within the field of education itself every educational researcher is familiar with the pressure from administrators to work on "important" problems.

I also suspect that there is another fundamental difference between those who do research on the periphery of education and those who identify primarily with education and who do research, so to speak, from the inside. Those looking at educational phenomena from the periphery regard them as natural phenomena to be investigated in much the same way as any other events are investigated. Discovering a general law or pattern from these events is done largely because it is fun to discover a law and to fit knowledge together into a pattern. On the other hand, those who identify closely with education see research as closely tied to the resolution of issues on which they have already taken sides. The results of research are not just objective finding but are supportive or damaging to positions already accepted. Sometimes they may be damaging to a position on educational practice which an educator has spent a lifetime attempting to promote. It is hardly surprising that research has not flourished under such conditions of high ego involvement where the dispassionate attitudes of the scientist probably cannot exist. The educator is a victim of circumstances in this matter. The very nature of the work which he undertakes makes him an integral part of the phenomena which the scientist from the outside may study, but his own participation in the phenomena of education limits his capacity to turn around and study these same phenomena. Perhaps it is much more than one can expect of a person to be both a participant in a phenomenon and a student of the phenomenon of which he is a part.

INDEX

Academy Movement, 135–38
Adams, Henry, 5, 142
Applied and pure disciplines, 164–68, 172, 180–83

Babbitt, Irving, 5
Bailyn, Bernard, 6, 125, 139
Bain, Alexander, 6
Baker, Sir Ernest, 7
Barnard, Henry, 132
Beard, Charles, 142

Communication: as a criterion of a discipline, 122
Concern of Education, 75–80, 83–84
Cubberly, Elwood, 127, 132

Dewey, John, 128–29
Discipline, 5, 62–65, 85, 101, 159
Discipline: administrative sense of word, 62–63, 149
Discipline of Education, 6–16, 38, 65, 102, 104–5, 120, 138, 150, 170–71; and teaching, 15–16, 20–21, 27–28; the theoretical basis, 49–61, 64–71; an applied discipline, 180–83

Ecology of Education, 156–57
Education, 5, 26; the subject matter, 6–20, 40, 71, 74–75, 92, 102, 151; and other social sciences, 8–10, 18–21, 78–80, 155–59, 167–83; as a profession, 22, 85–97, 150–52, 184–85; as an art, 48, 123–24, 147–49, 160–61; as a science, 59, 126, 179; and society, 73–74, 82

Educational phenomena, 51–54
Educational practice, 15–16, 47–48
Educational principles, 59–61, 84
Educational psychology, 78–80, 105–20, 169–70; and the practice of Education, 115, 118–19, 123–24
Educational Realm, 49–51
Educational Review, 126
Educational terms, 54–60, 67

Flexner, A., 87
Freud, S., 92

Goals: in teaching, 24; in Education, 83
Graduate study in Education, 151, 172

Hall, G. Stanley, 127
Hempel, C. G., 58
Higher Education in the 19th century, 134–35
History of Education, 131–39, 142–44, 170

James, William, 128
Journal of Educational Psychology, 107

Learning, 106, 109–13, 116, 123
Lynch, W. W., 114–15

Mann, Horace, 132–34
Mannheim, Karl, 8
Meehl, Paul E., 117

189